GITA

SPIRITUALITY FOR
LEADERSHIP & SUCCESS

Ultimate Spiritual Lessons,
based on the PowerTalks and MysticTalks of

PRANAY

BEL!EF

Reprint 2023

FiNGERPRINT! BELiEF

An imprint of Prakash Books India Pvt. Ltd.

113/A, Darya Ganj, New Delhi-110 002,
Tel: (011) 2324 7062 – 65, Fax: (011) 2324 6975
Email: info@prakashbooks.com/sales@prakashbooks.com

facebook www.facebook.com/fingerprintpublishing
twitter www.twitter.com/FingerprintP
www.fingerprintpublishing.com

ISBN: 978 93 9039 190 5

Processed & printed in India

Preface

Krishna's Bhagavad Gita has inspired leaders in every sphere of life. Science and Modern Warfare: J Robert Oppenheimer. Politics: Subhash Chandra Bose. Business and Technology: Steve Jobs. Philosophy: Emerson. And countless other luminaries over the ages.

During times of crisis, Krishna's life and leadership lessons become especially important! His tremendous insights within the Gita are the highest teachings for overcoming life's difficulties and tough times. In the face of pandemics and other challenges, leaders—and all those seeking true success—would do well to imbibe the Gita's powerful lessons.

The Gita is perhaps the most balanced mix of both the practical and the cosmically profound aspects of our existence. It is the 'art of war' as well as the art of inner peace. At its heart, the Gita contains a mystical code or set of fundamental principles related to warrior-hood and leadership *(netritva)* of all kinds, making it relevant and universal in a way no other text is. This book distils and presents some of the most important keys of the Gita's timeless lesssons for leadership and success.

Pranay

Contents

CHAPTER - 1

Understanding Dynamic
Change Is the Key

*LESSON: Krishna advises calmness amidst change.
This is key for leaders and for all those seeking true
success. It makes the core of your being more energetic,
pure, powerful, and dynamized. In a world going
through massive changes and unexpected situations
such as dangerous epidemics and economic crashes,
calm acceptance of change needs to be within your
consciousness. It leads to the ability to perceive with
clarity and act with one's highest energies awake. It
enables one to adapt quickly, thereby making one's
personal effectiveness far stronger.*

The Gita is fundamentally about the principle
of change. Change is inherent in existence. Very
clearly, Krishna is telling Arjun that all things are

dynamic. *Gatisheelta* or dynamism is inherent in existence. Nothing is static. And only by understanding the fundamental principle of change do we have the ability to cope with all change, all disruptions in the status quo, with great calmness.

This is a very important teaching for leaders at all levels. It enables higher achievement, progress, and prosperity for leaders and the people they lead. The understanding of dynamic change allows leaders to gauge the vital turning points for decision-making at crucial moments, thereby leading to greater chances of success.

The understanding of change leads to unattached and dynamic action, and overcoming fear of *what may or may not happen*. It is at the heart of the message of 'Karma Yoga' or the yoga of work that Krishna is instructing Arjun about: 'Arjun, perform actions giving up attachment, unconcerned as to success or failure!' This teaching is preparing Arjun to accept any change to what he had thought may be possible, and preparing him for any circumstance that may occur! It is a great secret for dynamic, fearless, and spiritually evolved leadership!

Nothing is permanent. There is no certainty about any material event or outcome: it is all subject to a greater power than the human. Yet we must act dynamically and happily even knowing this: that is the true spiritual approach to life and leadership. This is what Krishna continually advises Arjun. But he goes much further, showing Arjun cosmic changes within his universal form—with the continuous formation of stars, galaxies, nebulae, beings living and dying, the whole cycle of life and death continuing. So all things are dynamically changing, and the dynamic attitude of the leader needs to be one which understands that this change is the key. We have to change our mindset about things, just as Arjun changes his mindset.

The problem with religion is that it is often frozen in time: it has simply not evolved to keep pace with civilizational change. Maybe when it was propounded, by the original founders of the religion, it had meaning. But perhaps some of its tenets have outlived their expiration date! Hence, all that we know must be changed. The mind must first change in attitude, to be accepting of change. Then can we cope with change in the practical, material sphere.

People often get misguided by old concepts, frozen in their mindsets. Being frozen in attitude means there is no dynamic flow of perception, no new understanding. Leadership insight and leadership vision require a fresh flow of consciousness. Hence, allow your consciousness to flow into new understanding. Then only does every moment become intensely whole, then only does your understanding as a leader or as a team member become total. Else, you are as if on an island, a prison of old ideas. As if your very concepts have become your bondage. The problem with human beings is that for millennia we have lived with the promise of a utopia, a heaven after death, and so on. But that is not practical, because it gives us a very fixed and frozen view of existence. Whereas existence is a continuous creativity. And to move on with its dynamic flow, to change one's attitude to an attitude of creativity, is what it means to be able to cope with reality in the best manner.

Therefore, the best and most natural leaders are those who do not go by ideas of yesterday. Who do not go by inhibitions of what is 'taboo' or what is 'allowed'. They are always breaking the rules! They rebel against notions of the past. They rebel against codes of morality even, when need be. They disown any kind of mental resistance to change. And this is what they try and inculcate in their teams too. Yet they do all this with great calmness, because they are accepting of change.

For any society to evolve, for any team—or nation even—to evolve, there must be a mass consciousness of accepting positive change. Of going beyond the accepted structure, the accepted discipline. So, it's fundamentally about a change of mindset. Who has given us so many different kinds of moralities? Who has given us so many different kinds of dogmas? It is religion, it is society. And this is what has prevented us from being natural. The funny part is that it is only mankind who gets stuck in attitudes! Nature knows how to cope with change.

Nature evolves, constantly. But also remember that species in nature do get extinct: so in that way man too can become extinct, if he does not transcend his condemnation of change. Instead of condemning change, all religions should welcome change. Instead of condemning change, all societies should welcome change. To change positively is progressive evolution. What is evolution: outer evolution, inner evolution, evolution of the mind, evolution of consciousness? What is wisdom? Evolution is moving towards greater wisdom in a practical manner, so that survivability is ensured. But it also implies the dawn of greater intelligence for dealing with current situations and challenges facing us.

Krishna is telling Arjun very clearly to forget about his resistance to change. To forget about his old ideas, and to observe very correctly what is really going on at a universal level. He gives Arjun the eyes of insight, to look at how all things are in a dynamic flux. And that it is only by accepting the truth of dynamic flux that we have any hope of coping with change. It's like watching a play, a drama. We cannot keep repeating the same scene one after the other. One scene leads to the next, and so on. Such is life. So is the universe and this cosmic existence, so is our own evolution and our evolutionary requirement.

In the mystic and spiritual view, it is needed that you see what all the mystics have affirmed over centuries and over thousands of years. That we are not to get stuck in our mental positions, in our mental comfort zones or our orthodox styles of thinking. Because by doing that, you do not move on to the next stage of either spiritual evolution or mental evolution. And remember, there is an infinity of stages in the realm of consciousness. There is no place that after reaching you can say, 'Okay, I have made it! This is it!' There are realms and realms of consciousness to ascend to. Similarly, to move into something meaningful at a material level—to innovate, to help one's team innovate, to be creative—requires us to move into new ways of thinking. Into new ways of looking at problems. That is the secret, the key, which the world needs. To awaken to that is needed today! So that is the primary thing a leader needs to see, to examine: 'what is needed now?' And based on that clarity of vision—of what is needed—to work toward fulfilling that.

Each generation has its own pain points, and a good leader knows how to address those. If in the 1960s and '70s it was the threat of global nuclear catastrophe and Cold War politics (ushering in anti-war propaganda in the United States), in the 1980s it became one of rapid computerization, of taking technology to the masses. In the 1990s, it became more about globalization. And in this century, the most crucial situations facing us are not only human conflict, but also those of public health, ecology, and environment. So each generation brings its own pain points, and a good leader knows how to address those in the best possible manner, in a calm state of inner being. Leaving aside that which has been known in the past! Then only do the dimensions of oneself function to the fullest as a leader: on the material sphere, the mental sphere, and the spiritual sphere.

Make Self-Awareness Your First Priority

LESSON: Krishna is making Arjun think more about the inner 'self'. Through that, Arjun's thoughts stop running around uselessly. He is able to direct his life-force in a constructive manner, both towards fighting the war of justice externally, and realizing his inner reality spiritually. It is key for leaders to focus internally, as that purifies and empowers the consciousness: one does not waste energy on useless anxieties and thoughts. One is able to go past fear and mental obstacles, and do what needs to be done as a leader with more awareness and wisdom. This is important especially during crisis situations or tough times. It is a secret of charismatic and highly effective leadership. Internalization and self-knowledge are the bedrock of the Gita's leadership and success lessons.

Self-awareness should be the first priority of every human being. It's about putting one's energy into knowing who you are, knowing your very roots at the spiritual level. If that is going correct, then everything in your life goes correct. And that is a very central message of the Gita: to know your authentic self *(atmagyana)*. From that comes the energy to create excellence in whatever you do: whether you are a warrior, a leader, a professional in any field. For leadership, the attribute of true self-confidence is the most fundamental thing, and that is only born of deep self-awareness.

But usually, man's first priorities are absolutely different from self-awareness. They are position, power, ambition, and achievement. So there's a massive gap between one's ambition and goals, and self-awareness. And when this gap is too large, you have a case of the blind leading the blind. How many leaders have you seen who worked towards self-awareness with the totality of their energy? Perhaps very few. But those who do, become great leaders, become great warriors in the true sense.

Krishna is constantly reminding Arjun to find his *swadharma*: his self-nature, and function through that. That is the first priority. Everything that flows from that becomes successful in a deeper manner. So it is a question of being completely open and completely invested in the search for self-realization, for self-awareness. In that way, the entirety of human effort should be one of awakening your innate and innermost energies.

Self-growth at the deepest level of yourself should be the priority, and that is the whole function of the Gita itself. It is a symbol of coming back to the priority of your being, of developing the inner eye of intuition. And when you develop the inner eye of intuition, it becomes like a laser beam: very powerfully cutting through all obstacles.

On the battlefield of Kurukshetra, very few people have this search within themselves: of self-awareness. Everybody is fighting for a position, to win and so on. But if the first thing is not correct, the whole direction of the ambition goes wrong. If you are walking in the wrong direction at the beginning of a journey, you can never reach the real destination! In other words, you can never really achieve the aim of life. Of fulfilment, bliss, self-realization.

Krishna bring brings Arjun back to that which is the utmost priority. Arjun is only symbolic of mankind as a totality. Arjun is only symbolic of what we all should be doing. But we are so invested in the rubbish which our minds are feeding us—our thoughts of anxiety, our thoughts of fear, our thoughts of winning at something—that we are moving further and further away from our swadharma or the dignity of our self-nature. As we move away from it, we also move away from the meaning and purpose of life. And leadership without a true spiritual purpose cannot be expected to lead to anything beneficial.

All the good impulses of man flow out of the search for self-realization. Because that in turn intensifies your sense of insight, your sense of empathy and of self-power. There is no real power without your intrinsic and mystic self-power. If that is missing, your whole life becomes confusing. You see, most leaders are leading their people—their teams, their society, their nation, their community—into more and more confusion. The whole structure is built on sand, and a house built on sand (as Jesus also says) is sure to fall! Build your house on the rock of self-awareness, and then you will be living a truly fulfilling life as a team player and as a leader.

During the course of the Gita, Arjun constantly starts coming back to his real self-nature. He starts attaining the highest peaks of his awareness. And then his action becomes total! His action becomes transcendent to the individual self and its narrow aims. And when your awareness goes beyond your individual self, it starts having meaning in a broader dimension. It starts having meaning for society, meaning for others. Thereafter, you assume a natural leadership role, because your actions affect others more. Otherwise how can you be a leader? It is like a general on the battlefield: a general's purpose is to direct his forces. His motivations must be for the whole collective team, and not just to feed his sense of ambition. When his energy is invested in the good of the whole, then only does his action lead to a victory of all.

So essentially, the lesson is that we must work on ourselves, on our own beings. When you work on yourself with earnestness, all other work becomes spontaneously fulfilled. Because it flows out of your innermost life-force. And remember, self-awareness does not mean sacrificing action! In fact, it means an undercurrent of awareness no matter what you are doing: whether you are in the midst of a challenge, whether you are networking or communicating with others, and so on. No matter what you are doing, no matter what the project you are engaged in, there is to be an underlying stream of self-remembrance below the activity which is happening on the surface. You see, more than ninety percent of the mind exists in the unconscious and subconscious part of ourselves. Self-awareness simply means activating that unconscious and subconscious part of ourselves. And when we activate it, then what we are doing on the surface or at the material level becomes energized with the totality of our energy!

Our inner activity nourishes our outer activity. Mind and spirit shape all action. And when the inner being nourishes the outward activity with more self-awareness, the outward activity becomes more dynamic! Not only does it become more dynamic, it becomes more invested with sensitivity and insight.

Who is a great person or great leader? A great person is simply one who can activate the deeper levels of themselves in whatever they are doing. Through the very act of activating our inner consciousness, that which we are doing at the material level starts developing a greater quality and purpose. Your whole energy changes: instead of doing things mechanically, you do things with passion. And where there is passion, there is excellence.

Balanced Consciousness Vs. Disturbed Consciousness

LESSON: Balance is the foundation of true success and great leadership. Being balanced implies a relaxed yet intuitively awake capacity to not be afraid of any circumstances. It implies creation of a silent dynamo of energy within you, within which your emotions and thoughts are in a tranquil state. Being spontaneously cheerful, optimistic, and maintaining an attitude of friendliness—no matter what the odds—is key to finding balance. It leads to a far higher quality of both life and leadership success.

One of the most important things to understand for true success and effective leadership is that of being balanced *(santulit)* in one's consciousness. In fact, that is a central theme of the Gita itself.

The crux of the Gita is of having a consciousness which is completely balanced, calm, tranquil, in order, and in control. The kind of consciousness which Arjun displays in the beginning of the Gita is the opposite: it's a highly disturbed consciousness. Agitated, in turmoil, mentally in disorder. It is obvious that a warrior on the battlefield, especially one who is supposed to set an example for others, must display a balanced consciousness. Not only is it good from the point of view of achieving the task at hand—of winning the battle and overcoming the challenge—but it also creates a great respect for that person from the point of view of his team members and his fellow fighters. Krishna is constantly advising Arjun to find his balance. To find calmness within. And to simply get rid of the agitation in his mind, because that is the only way that our being will be positively nourished from within. And being positively nourished from within, he will be able to act in the correct manner.

Whatever happens out of a balanced consciousness is bound to be correct. Whatever happens out of a disturbed consciousness is bound to be incorrect, and leads to disastrous results. Very clearly, Krishna points out to Arjun that not only will he lose respect in the eyes of his fellow warriors if he remains so disturbed, but he will also not be able to come to a state where he functions with focus and concentration. For totality of action, it is really needed that one meets whatever circumstances that come one's way with a total of balanced awareness. So that nothing disturbs one. It is like a tightrope walker, walking the rope with the balancing pole. He has to cross that rope; he has to surmount the challenge. But if he becomes disturbed in his state of mind, he's bound to fall from that height! So, Krishna counsels Arjun that he is about to lose all that is good within himself simply because of being agitated.

Balance implies being able to look at a situation in a passive, non-judgmental way. Look at the situation with totality of consciousness, without the fog of conditioning or mental/emotional prejudice. And this is the kind of mindset which not only a fighter on the battlefield has to have, but also one that a leader in the midst of any action in the world should have. Because that is what leads to welfare of both the individual and society. Otherwise, one is completely in a situation which leads to turmoil in one's inner state. And turmoil in our inner psycho-spiritual state simply leads to turmoil in our material actions.

See how the mind is functioning: watch your own mind. Is it balanced? If it is, then no matter what the challenge, you can go into the challenge happily. You can go into the challenge with a transcendent awareness. And transcendent awareness means cutting away the non-essential, focusing on what truly needs to be done for the task! This is supremely important for a leader who seeks to make his team come to a totality of action, in order to achieve their desired result. But to make the concentration total, to make the focus like a laser beam, there has to be a situation where the mind is absorbed in a harmonious flow towards the task. If harmony of mental flow is lost, then the direction itself is lost. The energy is lost. And one reaches nowhere. It is then like water on sand: no matter how much you pour, it will still not flow.

So, make the consciousness like a clear path. On that clear path will come a clear and dynamic flow. And when the energy of consciousness flows with a dynamic clarity, then does it become unstoppable. Then what one is doing is not being done just because one has to finish the task, but it is being done with a feeling of inner ecstasy. With a feeling of inner meaning. Hence, the task itself becomes imbued and invested with meaning, and when that happens it has an effect not only on oneself but on the entirety of the team one is leading. Then do people feel hope, then do people feel, 'Yes, this is something in which we can be total in our dedication and energy!'

And if there is total dedication and energy from the team's side, then there has to come something good out of it! Your team may lose a battle but you can still win the war. Don't worry about the results, worry about the sense of balance which you need to bring unto yourself.

Because that changes the consciousness of all those who are leading. It is like the difference between the awakened state and the sleeping state: in the sleeping state, the mind goes helter-skelter, dreaming and imagining different things. You can have a nightmare. But if you are truly awake then the nightmare does not disturb you, because you know that there is a deeper reality. And that the dream is only a figment of your imagination. And most problems are in fact a figment of our imagination. You need to be in a state where you can forget about them, and simply focusing on the moments you have and the resources you have, you maximize your efforts.

The greatest generals on the battlefield have been able to exhibit this balance. The greatest sportsmen on the sports field have been able to exhibit this balance. It is not about talent alone; it is about specifically coming to a situation where the negative aspects of the mind have dissolved, the agitations of the mind have dissolved.

Gradually, as the Bhagavad Gita is expounded to Arjun, he comes to this state where all his doubts start dissolving. He brings his mind into a state of order, into a state of control. This state of self-control is the creative state. It is the state from which good things happen. From a state of disorder in consciousness, how can you expect things to happen in a positive manner? At the most, they will be a fluke.

So the principle of balance is a foundational one which applies to all things, and especially to leadership. Do not waste your effort by investing it in mental disturbances; invest your effort in balance, because that is the single best investment you can have as far as your being goes. That way, you go more deeply into yourself. And out of that depth, all negativities are uprooted. Leaving you with a straight and clear path, walking which you come to a limitless, boundless energy of the team. And most importantly, of yourself.

CHAPTER-4

Heartfulness and Intellect Must Combine for Real Fulfilment

LESSON: Great leaders know the ultimate lesson: how to combine peaceful inner feelings with empowering thoughts. Krishna's way is on the one hand about quietening one's inner emotions and feelings, and on the other hand bringing about the highest vibration of one's mind-body-spirit energies of thought and action. Through this combination he empowers Arjun, and enables him to lead by example as a warrior on the battlefield. This is a lesson for our own leadership and life 'battles' or challenges. It creates inner brightness within one's consciousness, and a charismatic appeal for those one leads.

The Bhagavad Gita is a unique text because it talks about fulfilment at every level: in the world of action and in the inner world. It always emphasizes both inner *(aantarik)* and outer *(bhautik)* richness, in order for us to act dynamically in whatever position we are in. To always keep an inner eye on the essentially spiritual and mystical aspects of existence. It constantly echoes the truth that intellect and heartfulness have to combine for true fulfilment in everything.

In other words, our mental impulses have to be strengthened by our deeper spiritual impulses. Then only do we achieve real and true success. You see, the intellect is good for the tasks we need to carry out in the world, and sometimes the heart is not a very good judge of circumstances and situations (especially for a leader). But without 'heartful' realization, insight does not happen.

One of the underlying factors of this sacred text is constantly bringing both approaches—of head and of heart—to bear on our roles as people of action, and as leaders within the world. Krishna is constantly telling Arjun that his approach has to be one of total vision. Then only will transformation come, then only will the consciousness change. But at the same time, he also tells him that it is very important for him to set an example in society as a doer of action. So it is a question of balancing both the impulses of the intellect as well as the mystical impulses of the heart. And the 'heart' is metaphorical: it does not mean the physical heart but rather our higher nature.

Mind itself is not capable enough to grasp everything. In fact, the more profoundly subtle and beautiful the experience, the less and less becomes the mind's level of insight into it. The outer layers of intellect are not as rich as our innermost and deeper consciousness. This is very important for leaders to understand: a lot of people lead with intellect, which is good, and there are some leaders who do not use intellect as much as the heart. They go by their feelings. But both approaches eventually cannot lead to ultimate truth. The deeper secrets of leadership have to be found in a balance between intellect and heartfulness. The richness of the inner must reflect the richness of the outer, and vice versa. Otherwise one part will remain poor.

There are very few leaders who exhibit proficiency in both aspects: intellectual as well as spiritual. And what does the spiritual impulse or the heartfelt impulse mean? It basically means that you must have an intensity of longing for truth. This is what Krishna is telling Arjun. You must be strong in your search! Thirsty in your search! Then only does your higher nature get awakened. Then only can you move on to gauging deeper truth. And the ability to gauge deeper truth is the hallmark of all great leaders. Without it, you do not evolve into being a leader of insight into objective reality. You live in dreams. So to know objective reality as it is, is the first step. Then only can you act with dynamism.

A good leader is hence to go into all situations with truly open 'eyes': eyes not only of the intellect, but the wisdom eye of the spiritual 'heart' or soul. That is the hidden eye, which is called in Indian mysticism the wisdom eye or 'third eye'. It implies the deeper intuitive intelligence-consciousness of ourselves. Our vision of things needs to begin from there. In other words, we are to become better, deeper observers, who can look at things in a more holistic, insightful manner.

What Krishna is trying to explain to Arjun is that basically all existence is a very mysterious phenomenon, suffused with the divine spirit, which He represents. But to open the secrets of this mysterious phenomenon called life, it requires us to surrender our mind to the greater reality. In fact, the concept of 'surrender' is at the key of the entire Gita itself. To give up your small intellectual ideas, and realize that there is an entire world to be discovered within you, of which the heart has an inclination. Of which your faith has an inclination. So really it is about a rediscovery of your essential nature. And the whole Gita is about a rediscovery of this hidden potential within yourself.

The divine echoes within us not only in our intellect but in our heart also. And a person who recognizes this echo starts becoming tremendously fulfilled. Starts becoming tremendously passionate and dynamic in their whole attitude toward life. The whole Gita deals not with specific teachings on leadership as such, but with those in the realm of 'consciousness', which are essentially the foundation for all great action and all great leadership. A leader is one who needs to have great courage, great honour, great nobility of action. That is what a great leader should be, and that is what the whole Gita is pointing towards. To make you more authentic in your potential; to make you come out of the pretence of conditioned thoughts; to lead you to such a kind of courage that you work unconcerned about name, fame, position, and so on. And only through this unconcerned utter abandonment and faith of the heart can a person scale the deepest heights of achievement.

The person who's constantly tied down by the limited concepts of the mind and the ego cannot really move on to a freedom of consciousness. And to be a truly great warrior or a truly great leader implies that you go beyond all limitations. Go beyond personal pride. Krishna breaks down Arjun's pride: only then does Arjun achieve true dignity as a warrior. He is telling Arjun that man is really an unlimited potentiality provided he recognizes that along with intellect, intuition is also to be used. Then only can we simultaneously achieve both inner and outer success. Discover the divinity within your own being: that is the ultimate secret of the text. And you can only discover it when you are prepared to go beyond the conditioned confines of thought, and enter the world of spirit and heartfulness which are the greatest parts of yourself.

Liberate Yourself from the Past

LESSON: Let go of all past worries. They make one heavy, unhappy, and less effective as a leader. True success and dynamic leadership begin with the ability to go past all past anguish and failures. That is the only way to generate enough energy to deal with current challenges and crisis situations. Going back to past anxious feelings creates mental weakness. Krishna shakes Arjun up from that, through the sublime teachings of the Gita.

Leadership is the art of being able to see what others cannot perceive, and acting on those insights with passionate drive. But how does one develop real insight *(pragya/antardristi)*? One develops insight by liberating oneself from one's past, liberating oneself from the known, from the mind's baggage of conditioning.

And in the Gita we find a very significant pointer to this: Arjun is looking at Krishna as a friend, and eventually he realizes that he is much, much more than his personal friend or his brother-in-law (they are related by marriage). He, Krishna, is the divine manifestation of the ultimate reality. And Arjun asks for forgiveness from Krishna when he sees the supreme form, the cosmic and universal form of His. So Arjun develops fresh 'eyes' with which to look at this new reality confronting him. And we must all develop fresh 'eyes' to look at things, in order to look insightfully into reality, whether we are leaders or team players.

Detach yourself from the past, and then only can you look at things and act as if you have a new being. It is almost like a rebirth of vision. In Hinduism it is called being *dwija*, born again. Your eyes then have an intensity of purpose, and your senses are alert. Most human beings have conditioned responses to situations, but true leaders do not. They do not rely on conditioned responses. They create an alertness of their senses, and only through alertness of one's senses does one develop the ability to work with true and ready intelligence. Readiness of intelligence, aliveness of intelligence is what distinguishes dynamic leaders from mediocre ones. Even when others are asleep, the leader's consciousness is awake, in a subtle manner. And that's why he or she is a dynamic leader.

The same principles which are applied to warrior-hood can be applied to leadership. And that is the whole metaphor of the Gita. A good warrior must have the same abilities which a good leader must have, and vice versa. The warrior cannot afford to be caught in his past, his anxiety, his thoughts about yesterday. He brings the totality of his energy into the fight, into the challenge confronting him. And that is why he is a good warrior. Otherwise he'd be a poor warrior.

The Bhagavad Gita is outwardly the mystical song conveyed by Krishna to Arjun, but actually it is the unsung song in our own hearts. Constantly, existence wants to sing that song within our hearts. And into our consciousness. To breathe it into our awareness. But we are not aware of it. We are all eventually an 'Arjun'. We forget he is only a metaphor for each of us as individual beings. And the voice of the divine—or in other words this *song* of the divine—constantly wants to be sung within us. But we have to be receptive to it. And to be receptive to it means liberating ourselves from whatever we have known. Being prepared to awaken to a new sense of looking into the universe, with a new sensibility. Only then do we understand the mystic chord. Otherwise everything functions through the chains of the past.

In essence, the Gita is about liberating us from our past Karmas, our mental accumulations. And the moment we awaken out of that dream of the past, is when we start feeling great freedom. The Gita has a great pragmatic value: while it talks about the mystic code, it also talks about how we can refresh our hearts and minds to function within the world. It has a great cleansing effect upon us as far as nourishing us for worldly action goes. That is why it is called the most significant sacred text and Krishna is called the 'Milker of the Upanishads', meaning he has taken the best of the Upanishads and condensed it into a work which shatters the ego. Which smashes the anxiety within us. Which nourishes us at a very deep level. Creating root-level courage in us. And at the same time, creating contentment and joy.

Krishna is telling us to completely drop our worried thoughts, our anxious thoughts. And dropping such thoughts requires us to leave the past behind, not dwell on it too much. It's very simple: you have to let go of it, only then can you move into spaces which are both mystically and materially dynamic. And that makes a complete leader: a person who can use the intuition of the mystic space within himself or herself, and be ready for any action which is required in the material space, both spontaneously and together. That is what is the ultimate lesson of the text. To be filled with hope; to not lose hope; to learn the art of serenity.

Our past has a firm grip on us: it keeps us in its

prison. It stops us from moving towards perfection. It creates a tension within us, it solidifies the ego within us. And without getting rid of the tension and the ego, no human being can evolve to greater heights. No matter what achievement a human being is looking for, to move with greater energy and to bloom to their utmost potential requires them in essence to flow out of the stuck past. Let it disappear. There is no harm if your past disappears from the spiritual perspective: do not let it be a distraction for you! Do not function out of an old mindset, rather be prepared for the new. Then only will you encounter new peaks of achievement. And a leader is somebody who helps others to climb new peaks of achievement. If a leader himself or herself is not relaxed enough and loose enough from the past, to create an immensity of energy in the present moment, how can she or he inspire others to follow on that path towards the summit?

Achievement is therefore like climbing a mountain. But to climb a mountain we must get rid of extra baggage, otherwise we will not be able to climb in a manner which rejuvenates us. Rather it will only tire us! So climb the heights of leadership with harmony in your heart, a song in your heart, the essence of the Gita's message in your heart. That is the essence of the mystic code of this sublime text gifted to us by the divine aspect of existence.

CHAPTER-6

Tenseness Makes You Narrow, Non-Tenseness Makes You Vast and Abundant

LESSON: Do not get tense due to circumstances. This is a fundamental tenet of Krishna's Gita. Through tenseness, you only restrict the infinite spectrum of your mind-body-soul energies. You have no limits at the spiritual level: realize your inner vastness and release yourself from the paralyzing grip of tenseness. Feeling oneself to be unlimited in soul is Krishna's prime teaching to Arjun. It enables Arjun to become relaxed yet intensely powerful in the fulfilment of his 'dharma' or spiritual duty as a warrior and leader. It is a lesson all leaders need to understand. Expand inwardly, and then your ability to be expansive and powerful as a leader increases manifold.

One of the main things to understand for both warriors and leaders is that when we become tense, we narrow ourselves. And narrowing ourselves, we miss the abundance which is available to us.

This is a very important principle in the Gita: Arjun as a warrior and a leader on the battlefield is extremely tense, and due to this his mind has become very narrow and bewildered. Very caught up in his problem. So Krishna works on making him non-tense. And as the Gita is expounded by Krishna, Arjun attains a state of non-tenseness. A great feeling of freedom and abundance comes to him. He finds energy overflowing into him. He finds that his potential can be put to good use. So this is a very basic principle not only for mysticism, but also for leadership and in all practical situations.

Tenseness makes us lose our skills, lose the potential of our skill set. It does not give us clarity. It does not give us the ability to see into the interior truth of things. We are not wise in our decision-making through it. We are not good at distinguishing between things when we are in a state of tenseness. We become very tunnel-visioned, not able to see the larger picture. And just as the example of Arjun is, so too is the whole path of leadership: being able to see the larger picture.

The leader in fact is somebody who can see the largest picture amongst his or her peers. Of course, details are important in everything, but *leadership vision* means being able to grasp the essential principle or the larger picture. And so doing, the leader can guide his or her team toward success. So that is what the state of non-tenseness does.

For a warrior on the battlefield this is a key principle. It is through his very state of tenseness (prior to hearing the Gita), that Arjun is not able to fight. He feels that his body and mind both are completely weak! He puts down his bow. The whole point is: we lose strength in a state of tenseness, we lose grace, we lose the vastness of our minds, we miss that which is available. And the whole search of fulfilment means to become more and more abundant with whatever is available, which only happens in a non-tense state of awareness.

This is a very fundamental law. It is really all about surrendering to whatever circumstances life brings us, without resistance: be vulnerable before any circumstance, but never be narrow, never be tense. Because your intelligence deserts you in such moments. Look into the 'eyes' of the problem confronting you, and then you will find it becomes solvable. Krishna confronts Arjun with the question of Arjun's sense of hopelessness, his sense of being utterly despondent. Arjun feels like there is no hope left at all in his life. He's on the verge of almost leaving everything. But leaving everything means an abandonment of your leadership position. It means you are not able to instil a good example for others on the battlefield of life. And that is not the spiritual way.

The spiritual way is that you do your actions in a relaxed manner: no matter whether you are fighting a battle or doing an intellectual task. The relaxed mind is always more open to truth. Which is why in life situations of any kind, this principle applies. You can recollect the story of Archimedes, the great Greek scientist and mathematician. He was unable to find a solution to a very critical problem regarding buoyancy, but one day while relaxing, having a bath in the tub, he had his so-called 'Eureka' moment! And so too have many other great people found that it is when they are in a very relaxed state, and in fact in unexpected states of being, that answers have come. People have made profound insights and discoveries in moments which were not necessarily moments of great concentration. Because sometimes concentration itself creates a state of tenseness. And that is a problem in today's world. Children, for example, are constantly being prodded into concentrating on their studies, doing homework and so on; but sometimes that creates a great stress within the child, leading to burnout. In the world of today, a lot of young professionals are burning out rather early into their careers. It is a question not of their skill-set, it is not a question of their ability. It is more a question of what is happening at their innermost core.

So if at the innermost core you are functioning out of tenseness, how can your outer actions be dynamic and flowing? The process and inspiration for action is also a subject of mysticism and not just of psychology. In what state of being you are in, is the key question. It is not just about the result of the action; it is the *process* itself which is important. And the process always means the inner intention, the interior driving force. The interior driving force should never be one of tension.

Krishna gives Arjun a higher driving force, and from that point Arjun starts feeling fresh. As if he is having a new life, as if he is making a new beginning. And he wakes up from his despair, as if he's fresh. He lifts his bow and gets ready to fight as the warrior he is. So too, as a leader, you must motivate others also within the team to work out of non-tenseness. There are some leaders who create a constant tension within teams, but that is not the noble way. Because that only leads to a cramping of individual style, a restriction of the potential of the team. Liberating the team means on the one hand giving them the structure to do the work, to have discipline, but on the other hand to also have space for the inner silence of the individual. So that they can tap into whatever is the finest in them. So that they can work in a state into which they bring their larger intelligence to bear upon the problem. That way, you will find the team members coming up with profound observations and insights, profound creativity.

Creativity and innovation always need a fresh state of being. A state where you are relaxed. This is also echoed in the Zen philosophy of Japan, which Steve Jobs of Apple Computer used to emulate. It implies a very relaxed way of life, yet a very alert and aware one at the same time! It is not the tense mind, but the relaxed mind which brings fulfilling results. A mind which is alive with awareness.

Hence, both things together—simultaneous relaxation and alert readiness for action—create a very powerful combination. This is what Krishna eventually instils into Arjun. And this is what every leader—and every person seeking true success—must seek to emulate.

CHAPTER - 7

Bliss Links Us, Despair De-Links Us

LESSON: 'Ananda' or bliss is the greatest human capacity. It is the fundamental quality of the whole universe, and exists within you as your highest reality.

Bliss is the causative factor of the cosmic matrix: manifest it more and more in all your life and leadership roles. It simply requires you to feel yourself as pure bliss, joy, delight: 'Ananda Swarupa' or 'Sukh Swarupa'.

Positive leadership implies such leadership that joins people together, connects people together. That is the essence of good teamwork. That is the part a leader must play. And the greatest glue to join people together is that of bliss and joy. If that is the attitude in a group, then it becomes united, it becomes strong in a positive way. What

Krishna is telling Arjun is that eventually, even for the individual to join with the Divine, what is needed is the glue of joy: because that is the strongest bond which can happen between two entities.

Yes, at several times leaders try and join people through finding and identifying a common enemy. That is what all fascists have done in history, Adolf Hitler being a prime example. He identified an enemy in the Jews, and he joined or united people in a negative manner against them, in order to secure his own pole position as leader of the German Reich. But eventually, the result of such 'unity' between people does not lead to anything good. It cannot lead to the joy of people. It cannot lead to happiness. It only leads to sorrow, to destructiveness.

The act of the positive leader, on the other hand, is to sow seeds of joy. That is real leadership virtue. The whole universe is said to be a product of the ultimate bliss of the Divine. That is the whole symbolism of Krishna playing his flute, beckoning and attracting others through His very bliss!

Let's look at team dynamics. What joy does is that it relaxes people with each other. And when people are relaxed with each other, they become more capable of creating something valuable together. They get together for a beautiful cause, and make it possible. All that seems impossible is a product of despair. Hope and optimism is a result of deep confidence and deep positive energy. And that is only possible when the mind has been cleansed and purified through the act of catalyzing mental joy, or through the stimulus of joy. It is the ultimate cleanser of heart and mind; it creates a deep confidence in people. And this confidence is one which is not egoistic in nature, but rather is about self-belief along with belief in others. Through such belief comes about heart-to-heart connection, mind to mind connection. And isn't that what positive team dynamics is supposed to mean?

Problems in teams stem primarily from too much distrust between team members. Distrust is a product of doubt about each other, and doubt is created when the group energy is not wholehearted in its vibe of joy. So for the team to flow in a natural manner—with dynamism and energy—requires a great open-mindedness. Joy creates this open-mindedness, and it is unlimited! It can go to infinity! There is no reason for it to be limited: it is always available in the depths of our being, to take us higher and make us stronger. The whole concept of creating a 'paradise', of creating a 'heaven', is one which is about inner spiritual impulse. And that spiritual impulse is the feeling of bliss.

These are things we have forgotten in our day-to-day lives. We seem to forget the key lesson for life and leadership: the joy of mutually shared respect. We live in a world of aggression, of competitive behaviour. Competition is healthy, but not a feeling of vengefulness. And in fact this is a very dramatic lesson in the Gita, where Krishna never advises Arjun to *hate* the enemy. Because out of such hatred, the greater purpose cannot be served. It would just create a pathological fear between people. And this becomes the barrier to optimum living.

Eventually, spirituality is all about living in one's most optimum state. That can only come about if you transform all negativities and channel them toward something positive. And the most positive thing is bliss, is joy. Fear disappears in the face of bliss! Darkness disappears, and one becomes full of light internally. And it is this inner light which gets expressed in the world of action.

The so-called 'real' world is not very distinct from our own psychological and spiritual state. The world is a reflection of how we are deep within. If we are calm and joyful deep within ourselves, our interactions with others too become full of calmness and joy. We are able to raise the energy of others, and so doing we spontaneously become positive leaders. No matter what our position is, no matter what our circumstances are.

Therefore, get rid of the conditionings of 'dislike' of others, fear of others. And move toward a situation where you are able to create a joyful vibration, no matter what group you are in: it could be a business team, it could be a sports team, it could be an army unit. When there is trust and joy with each other in the team, you are able to meet any challenge.

In a way Krishna is telling Arjun that if he is in a state of despair—which is the opposite of joy—how can he expect his fellow warriors to come to any state of fearlessness and real warrior-hood? They will also fall into despair, seeing the leader become full of despair (Arjun was after all one of the prime and principal players in this war, this battle). The whole energy and group dynamic of this army will become far lower than its potential. So, nothing good can come about in terms of the battle they are to fight. First, the feeling of 'enmity' is to disappear, but it can only disappear through the doorway of bliss and joy. Enter that door, and most of our psychological and spiritual dilemmas in life become solved.

There is a saying, 'Smile and the world smiles with you': so you create your world! If you are not blissful, don't expect others to follow you with bliss. But if you are blissful, you will find people attracted to you. Because that is your greatest treasure: people are simply attracted to the vibe and feel of joy! And people who can radiate such joy, can evolve into truly natural and spontaneous leaders.

The Crux of Spirituality Is Non-Possessiveness

LESSON: Krishna is taking Arjun towards a free and detached state of being! And when one is in such a state, one becomes fearless and immensely dynamic. What is there to fear when there is no sense of possessiveness? The seed of non-possessiveness creates greatness within our life and leadership roles. This is especially important during difficult situations or tough circumstances, such as the one Arjun faces.

One of the main points and essential meanings (*saar* in Sanskrit) of the Gita is that all possessiveness is pointless. Possessiveness restricts us, and stops us from being dynamic. The Bhagavad Gita says that we are to let go of possessiveness *(adhikaratmakta):* to our body, our attachments, our relationships, and most importantly to our actions. And to the result of our actions. This is extremely important from the leadership perspective!

Only through non-possessive action does true dynamism happen. Else, we are in constant anxiety, we are in constant worry. And eventually, worry and anxiety are what restrict our human capacity, our leadership capacity.

What does possessiveness do? You would have seen it in your own life: it only causes injury to you, it only causes disappointment to you. Spirituality is all about the consciousness that anxiety is meaningless, all worry is meaningless, because eventually we have to succumb to the material reality of death. We are at the mercy of larger cosmic forces in life. Yet people keep worrying. And this worry stems from possessiveness. If possessiveness can be let go of and dropped, you will find yourself attaining a deep inner coolness of being. You will become undisturbed, just as Arjun becomes undisturbed through listening to the divine words of Krishna. This is the essence of the Gita, and it is the crux of the spiritual and mystical search.

How the Gita is unique is that it professes no moral teaching. Its teachings are practical: both at a material and at a spiritual level. It says, live your life authentically and fully, but with the consciousness that non-possessiveness is the way forward, if at all you are to attain the state of real success as a warrior-leader. That is the mystic essence. A warrior who is too concerned about his attachments and his possessiveness of different things: relationships, sense of victory or defeat and so on, becomes too anxious to be able to fight with dynamism. And that is what Krishna is telling Arjun: you are to transform your energy and open up your awareness into non-possessive action which is unconcerned about results. That way, you become free, not only at the spiritual and mystical level but you also become free to act materially. And that is the hallmark of great leadership. Essentially what it means is that we require a correct atmosphere for our life energy to thrive in. And the sense of possessiveness does not help create the right mental atmosphere. It makes us feel fearful, it makes us tremble. Just as Arjun was trembling.

In the Gita, the description of Arjun trembling is a very poignant one. He is distracted. And how is he distracted? He is distracted primarily through this burden of possessiveness: he's possessive about his relationships, he's possessive about his ideas of right and wrong, of conscience. He's possessive about his prognosis of what will happen after the war. And all Krishna is telling him essentially is to completely let go of this pervasive sense of possessiveness. Because he, Arjun, is simply part of the universal ocean, and being a part of the universal ocean he just has to flow with its waves. This ability to flow with the large dimension is what dynamism and leadership is. If a person becomes capable of understanding this, something deep within is awakened. You suddenly become transformed in consciousness! Because then you feel yourself unlimited.

The main essence of truly great leadership is the sense that you are unlimited. That is what leads to real self-confidence. That is what leads to charismatic leadership. Feeling unlimited, you become fearless, you become courageous. Your decisions become very energetic. Something luminous starts growing within you, and people are attracted to this inner luminosity. All anxiety disappears, and once anxiety disappears you become a master of consciousness. And eventually to attain mastery of leadership, we need mastery of consciousness.

Spiritual well-being does not require you to climb the ladder of renunciation or asceticism. What it really requires of you is to become aware in the moment of a few key things, and knowing those few key things you find yourself suddenly free! You find that suddenly all the doors of existence have opened to you. It's a very liberating feeling, and this is the kind of liberation which Krishna always emphasizes: teaching Arjun that it is all about discovering within you that space which is vast, not limited by a sense of possessiveness. About having such courage that you can be trustful of existence itself, and so doing become energized at the level of heart and mind. Through this process, not only do your thoughts become less obsessive with the unnecessary, but you find yourself being able to fly into the higher realms of consciousness, which is what the meditative state of being means, no matter what you are doing.

These reasons are why the Gita is called the ultimate sacred text, because while it teaches you a practical mode of life, the essence of it is this mystic chord which runs through it. And the mystic chord is really the emphasis on the most significant and life-transformative aspects of living. The experience of bliss, the experience of opening up with courage to existence and releasing your energy to its maximum possible—that is what the Gita is constantly reminding us to do. And the only reason we are not able to release our complete energy into the world is because we are bound down by the chains of mental possessiveness. So let the spring break forth from yourself, let the fountain of the divine nectar go forth from yourself! But that only happens when you can unlock it by removing the rock of possessiveness which you have placed over it. Non-possessiveness is like bringing a light into a dark room: suddenly you find that your being does not need to be dictated by others. Suddenly you find that you can have a deep sense of being integrated and strong within yourself. Because there is nothing to fear when you get rid of possessiveness.

The hidden centre of existence is also hidden within you, as your core of being. But you don't discover it because you are too involved with your sense of possessiveness. It is not the position you possess, or the wealth you possess: in fact, possessions are not the problem, the problem is only the sense of ownership or possessiveness itself. Once you get rid of that, you become intense and passionate in your action. And that—at the foundational level—is what great leadership means.

The Gita Destroys
Self-Importance and Ego

LESSON: Krishna laughingly shatters the ego of Arjun. Suddenly, Arjun is able to see clearly that ego is the real barrier on the road to our highest success, realization, and happiness! Ego wounds our psyche, creating unnatural blockages in the flow of our energies. Cultivate a devotional and non-egoic attitude within your being: this is Krishna's highest message. This is very crucial for leaders to understand, as egoism is a common weakness of leaders. It only leads to a wastage of one's life and human potential. Let go of it, now. You will become light, happy, empowered, and immensely more capable by doing that!

A very important aspect of the Gita for leadership is that it completely destroys the sense of self-importance or ego *(ahankaar),* which is a common problem with leaders. Seeing oneself as the 'doer' of all things (instead of an instrument of the higher) is the root of egoism. Krishna tells Arjun, 'He whose mind is deluded with egoism thinks "I am the doer".'

On the battlefield of Kurukshetra are gathered all the great warriors from all the parts of the globe or of the civilized world. So says the Mahabharat. And being leaders of people, as well as great warriors, several of these people are filled with ego. They are fighting from an egoistic point of view. They are trying to dominate. They are trying to establish their importance and their power as leaders. But what Lord Krishna does is that He shows Arjun that eventually no human being is important in the cosmic scheme of things. Krishna assumes his supreme and ultimate form. That form within which Arjun can very clearly see all these great leaders and warriors go into the mouth of the Lord. All going towards death. And the Lord laughs, telling Arjun that eventually the human being is only an instrument of His bidding. We need to drop our egoism and realize greater cosmic spiritual truth as the 'doer', and not just our own limited selves.

The problem that has happened in religion and in leadership both, has been that man has taken upon himself a very central role: he feels he is the most important thing in existence! And by showing how insignificant human beings are in the scheme of the universe, the Lord shows Arjun that greatness must begin with simplicity, with humility. Out of this understanding of simplicity and humility comes real understanding. And out of such real understanding, does one become greater.

So, man becomes greater by understanding that he is not to fight from a position of ego or of position, of self-importance, but simply by being an instrument of the vaster existence. This is tremendously important. Because to be a truly great leader requires a depthful understanding: that we are only witnesses to a great cosmic play. So doing, we find our own individuality in the scheme of things. And finding our individuality, our true persona comes out in our actions. If we understand this fundamental mystic aspect of existence, then does our intelligence flower to its real potential. Then does the resurrection of our being happen to a degree where we realize that as instruments of existence we are real diamonds, but if it comes to ego we are simply dust! Because existence can destroy us any minute!

The Lord suggests that Arjun drop his sense of personality, ultimately of being a prince even, and be a completely vulnerable human. And being vulnerably human means to begin understanding and coming closer to one's real spiritual centre and core. By becoming closer to one's spiritual centre, a new consciousness arises within oneself. Then does a person become a positive contributor to the world.

Mankind has destroyed nature; mankind has taken it upon itself to feel like the greatest thing on earth! And so doing, there has been environmental degradation of all sorts. Exploitation not only of our fellow men, but of all the beings and of the ecology which coexists with us upon this beautiful earth. And these problems have manifested even more in the modern age, which is why the Gita's message of understanding one's rightful place is a timeless one for the modern age. Leaders have now, more than ever, to realize that they have to carry a sense of responsibility towards nature and towards all things. Towards preserving the environment. Towards being compassionate to their fellow human beings. Only out of that does the transformation of their leadership quality happen. Otherwise they are only acting out of ego, and they are becoming destructive. So the warrior, like the leader, is to understand that he is fighting only as an instrument of the Lord, and that at any moment he can be gone and destroyed. In such a state of consciousness does the wellspring of creativity and of real spiritual power manifest more strongly and arise within man. Man feels himself to be a more trusting and intimate part of the mystic aspect of existence. And so doing, he starts behaving in a manner which is more humble yet more powerfully connected to his environment. More conscious of other people, more conscious of the responsibilities he has been given by virtue of the position he holds. This is a mystic teaching of all religions, but it is condensed in a magnificent way in the Bhagavad Gita.

Krishna works very hard to destroy the sense of self-importance which Arjun has. Arjun is thinking that *his* problems are all-important, *his* anxiety is all-important. But Krishna shows him that eventually it is the original source of existence only which is important, and that we are only actors in this entire interplay of forces. Then does the intensity of Arjun's real spiritual will arise.

Spiritual will has a tremendous force, much more than mental will, much more than physical prowess. Because it is the foundational aspect of our consciousness. The lesson eventually is that we are here upon earth to celebrate the splendour and glory of existence, but we seem to have forgotten it by acting out of egoistic action. To appreciate in a spontaneous manner that we have been blessed with a great treasure with life upon earth, is to start becoming a much more responsible and yet a more simple leader. Simplicity is very important. Taking away the unnecessary parts which are limiting us. And the most unnecessary parts are those of false pride and ego. Because they only take us away from essential reality. They do not satisfy the desire for truth and fulfilment, which is the essence of human living.

Krishna is constantly making Arjun into a more watchful observer of existence and its laws. Of its deeper laws. He's cleansing Arjun's mind of all concepts of self-importance. And so doing, He is refreshing and nourishing Arjun's mind with a greater power and a greater wisdom.

Imbued with such understanding, the warrior's action starts flowing from a purer and more powerful state of being, full of more consciousness. And of far greater ability to do what is right and proper. To do that which is one's truest expression of self. If a person can express himself truly, then his or her potentiality comes to a real fruition, whether as a leader or in any other human role.

CHAPTER-10

Joy Is Our Natural State

LESSON: The trajectory of the Bhagavad Gita is of Arjun moving from joylessness to joyfulness. Only through inner joy does Arjun become the highest sort of leader on the battlefield. This is a lesson for you to absorb deep within your heart, especially when you are faced with difficult challenges.

All the religions of the world have, at heart, emphasized one thing: Know Yourself! It is not about knowing oneself at just the biophysical or mental level, but really the emphasis is on being your truest self as you are deep within. And at the heart of the Gita itself is the teaching, at a subterranean level, that we are essentially *pure and infinite joy (paramananda)* in our most natural self. The entire effort of Krishna is to bring Arjun to this natural state of liberated joy, so that he can act with dynamism! That is the basis of dynamic, effective, positive, and successful leadership: the way of the warrior.

What Arjun is experiencing is alien to his real nature of joy. Arjun is identifying himself with this alien nature of confusion and misery, which is the opposite of the natural joyful nature. Arjun falls more and more into confusion, more and more into his own misery. The remedy, the Gita tells us, is to remember that we are pure joy, and act out of that. It's a very simple thing: joy is our natural state, but that is what everybody forgets in the so-called real world, because we've forgotten to hear the inner silence and the inner melody. Which is the very essence of our being. It is simply within us, but outer anxiety makes us miserable. And being miserable, we act not as ourselves but through the workings of thought. And the workings of thought cannot by themselves lead to a state of joy. Thoughts can lead to logic, thought can lead to understanding a concept in principle, but thought can also lead to confusion and dogmatic thinking. All the religious fanaticism in the world is created through following a 'creed' or an 'ideology'. But no creed or ideology can by itself give us joy. The essential thing is to remember our natural state.

How is this important from the point of view of

leadership and success in the real world? It is in fact the most fundamental and important thing. Because without realization of our deeper natural state of joy, that which comes from us is meaningless and robot-like. Because it does not reflect us at our deepest levels. The real wisdom of mysticism and the real wisdom of spirituality lies in the teaching of joy. This liberates you, this takes you much further than being a mere biophysical machine which has to accomplish a 'task'.

The problem is that in most real world situations— be it the world of business organizations, the world of political outfits, that of academia or any other field which requires human action—you can see clearly that people are becoming more and more reduced into machine-like accomplishers of specific tasks. In so doing, they forget their intrinsic and basic qualities. But the emphasis upon our basic and intrinsic qualities is really what *reveals ourselves to ourselves*. And then do we feel blessed! A person who knows himself or herself to be pure joy, feels gratitude and feels blessed. Feels a great dynamic force within! And that is the very basis, the very pivot, for letting loose your highest potential.

Right through our education system and our societal conditioning, we are continually told that we should emulate certain other people. That we should be like them. This is the most pernicious teaching, because what it does is, it takes us away from our essential selfhood and individual naturalness of joy.

Eventually, the catalysts to evolving in life are questions which stimulate our own individuality, our deepest self-nature. That is the pith and meaning of the words of the Gita.

My interpretation of the Gita is not based on quoting it, but instead on finding the *essence of it; of distilling the most essential life and leadership lessons from it.* In that manner, I have found that the whole dialogue between the two principal actors in the Gita is that of creating a deep-rooted joy in the disciple. Krishna takes away all the confusion and anxiety which is preventing Arjun's joyful energy from flowing into his task at hand. And when all that is taken away, what remains is a hopeful, ecstatic, joyful state. Arjun eventually becomes full of great energy, and goes ahead to be his highest self on the battlefield. And that is essentially what every leader must emulate.

So for your own team members, it becomes important for you as a leader to take away their sense of anxiety. To take away their sense of dread, the sense of trepidation. To remove the negative qualities in the team, including worry, fear, anger, jealousy, procrastination, confusion, and so on. All this can be imbibed if we emulate Krishna to some degree, being somewhat of a spiritual guide to others. Not in an absolute or imitative way. But essentially by realizing that what a leader needs to do is to remove the anxiety which may be within the minds of the people whom one is leading. And if you do that, you start brightening the natural intelligence of your team, deep within the individuals in your team. When the essential intelligence quotient of a team gets brightened, you find it becoming extremely dynamic!

What is real intelligence in a spiritual sense? Intelligence begins by understanding that without a joyful energy, one is really going nowhere. The unjoyful state of being simply does not generate enough energy to create real value in the world. It is simply airy-fairy, because it does not appeal to the highest and the deepest within man. If you want to take out what is best within the individuals in your team, always remember what you have to give them—the vision to see that deep within, they each have the capacity to work with creative joy, creative abandon. So doing, you awaken their unconscious reserves of energy.

Therefore, a great leader awakens the unconscious reserves of joyful energy which are inherent within individuals. So doing, he makes them live and work in a much more intense manner than they have been doing. And eventually, thereby the team's goals become much easier to attain!

Arjun Is Chosen for Purity and Courage

LESSON: Where there is purity in consciousness, a spontaneous courage arises in one. Create purity in consciousness by having a loving attitude in life. This generates great courageousness to face all life situations as a leader. The amazing power of love is the highest power within you: all spiritual paths begin and end with it. In Krishna's vision, 'prema' or love creates self-fulfilment and dharma-fulfilment. History's most loved and respected leaders realized and shared great love, and thereby touched the lives of millions. They also fulfilled their intrinsic human potential of purity and courage through it.

One of the mysteries of the Gita is: why is Arjun chosen to receive the message from the Lord.

Is it only because they are great friends? Fundamentally, Arjun is chosen for his purity *(shuddhi)* of heart and mind. And more than anything else, is chosen for his purity of courage *(saahas)*.

Arjun has the courage to encounter the truth which the Lord is talking about. The fundamental truth, that which is life-transforming. And this courage to know the truth and act upon it, is the real quality of a spiritually grounded leader and warrior. It is almost like Arjun has those qualities within him which allow an inner transformation, because the essential qualities required for inner transformation are courage with purity.

Arjun also has the ability to walk on new paths, to encounter the new. To be able to absorb the new is primarily what courage is about. So this is a very essential part of the entire Gita. Courage is required to receive the cosmic vision which Arjun does from Krishna, as it is very mind-shattering.

The whole message of Krishna in the Gita is like a sword cutting away Arjun's doubts. Cutting away his sense of individuality and sense of ego. But to receive that sword of truth, only Arjun is capable on that battlefield of Kurukshetra. And that is the mystic message about why Arjun is chosen. Yes, there are moments during it when Arjun becomes fearful. But overall, he is able to retain his calm and cool demeanour.

A great leader or a great warrior is somebody who even while encountering something fundamentally new or challenging, is still able to gather together a great deal of coolness and calmness. This needs cultivation of inner integrity and inner unification of courage. Of not being broken or shattered by the external. Of internally being able to retain coolness and calmness. There is eventually no greater quality in an authentic leader than the ability to face things with calmness. That brings a transformation of potentiality into reality. Yes, everybody does have the capacity to be courageously calm and cool, but very few are able to focus this into constructive things.

Usually, battle or war is associated with people who have a certain degree of ruthlessness within them. But Arjun is not like that: he is not completely ruthless. He has doubts about killing others. He feels a lack of energy when it comes to hurting others if he feels it is not just. Yet he is able to ultimately pull this energy together and channel it in a very pure way, becoming an instrument for the cause of justice, for the larger good. And that is what the great leader is: a person who can gather courage for the cause of justice, making his inner self full of light, sensitive and pure enough but never surrendering his bravery! He is not fighting to dominate others or to take away their possessions. So in that way, he is not fighting out of a selfish end. And a great leader is somebody who is not to fight for a completely selfish end, but whose cause is greater than his own narrow self. Such a leader is the adventurous and rebellious leader who can lead others to good.

Throughout history, you will find that it is those leaders who have a backbone of steel but at the same time a pure heart, who live on as legends. There have been many conquerors, but very few who are considered noble. And it is this essential nobility of character—which implies both purity and courage—which is the very backbone of Arjun.

In order for humanity to develop to a new consciousness, and for its sensibility of leadership to develop to a new consciousness, we are to be very alert of these two qualities together. Courage without purity is of no use; purity without courage does not lead to the greater good.

And this is something you can notice with leadership of all levels. Just look at the basic school level: there are some children who when appointed as prefects or captains of their school, have a sense of courage but also purity of motivation. They can be relied on to do the right thing. So too does Krishna entrust Arjun with His divine message and His divine power, because He knows it will not be misutilized. So, existence gives more and more insight and power to those who can combine both these aspects—of purity and courage.

You can observe it in a business situation. Those people who earn real respect have the courage to do the right thing, to take the cause of humanity further. In our modern age, Elon Musk of Tesla is a very good example of this. He commands a different level of respect from others. He is extremely courageous in his ventures, but at the end of it people do associate with his pure ideal of serving humanity: whether it is through the electrification of vehicles or his vision to colonize other planets for the greater good of mankind. There are people in the world richer than him, but perhaps very few have commanded the level of respect he commands. And this is something which Krishna tells Arjun, this question of being respected in society, of earning true respect by fighting for the cause of justice. By not shirking away from the fight or running away from it. But at the same time, not misutilizing one's energies as a warrior or a leader. So, the negative is missing from Arjun's mind and Krishna knows he can entrust him with His message: to a degree where Arjun will take it further, to not only understand the truth of existence for himself but utilize it for fighting a battle which must be fought on the side of good. This is evolutionary leadership.

The other way is to go backward: where raw courage can be utilized to conquer, dominate, and possess what other people have. In the Mahabharat, the ideal example of it is Duryodhana. He is not lacking in courage; in fact, he is a very brave warrior. But he will not be chosen by the divine for the sublime message, simply because he cannot be trusted with such power of understanding which is meant to lead to the good of others.

A person of growth is a person who has more feelings for human beings, and, in fact, Arjun's feelings for his fellow warriors—even though they're his enemies—are born out of pure motivations. Because he does not want to utilize his courage and his skills as a warrior for chauvinistic purposes, or to dominate his opponents. The idea of killing them is anathema to him. It is not that he wants to be more powerful: he is not on a *power trip* of any kind. And that is a very essential teaching of the Gita. Those leaders who get into power trips will not be entrusted by existence to move towards self-fulfilment, but one such as Arjun will move not only towards victory or *jaya* in the battlefield of Kurukshetra, but will also move towards a victory in life. Towards contentment, towards spiritual realization, towards real fulfilment of his potential. Such people are able to channelize and concentrate their energies like a laser beam into doing something which allows them to become channels for greater good. They become mediums for greater good.

And when a leader decides or chooses to become a channel for greater good by becoming more pure and courageous in his or her motivations, he or she becomes unstoppable.

Religion Is Not Important, Mystic Vision Is

LESSON: Krishna's mystical vision belongs to every being: it is up to us whether to heed it or not. Cosmic consciousness goes beyond institutions of religion, and carries the amazing message of infiniteness. Sri Aurobindo describes the Gita as a living gospel: this implies that we are to understand it as a conveyor of ecstatic, infinite energy and not a religious book alone. Going into the Gita with this spirit enables us to appreciate its universality and optimism during the toughest circumstances—an attitude that is vital for leaders to imbibe.

The beauty of the Gita is that it clears up several things about religion as well as leadership *(netritva)*, while presenting a holistic vision that encompasses both the practical and the mystical aspects of life.

Krishna is not preaching 'religion' as such to Arjun. All he is doing is turning Arjun's face to the mystic or spiritual vision, to the heart of spirituality. And through that, Arjun's higher nature gets activated! It is really about how to raise the individual to his or her higher nature, and that cannot be done with 'religious ideology' as such. It is always shaped by what the individual's original world view and mystic vision is.

Throughout the Bhagavad Gita, Krishna is giving Arjun the mystic eyes to see that which is the highest form of spirituality. He's showing Arjun what real devotion is, what respect for values is, what true humanity means, and what our cosmic reality is. These are all mystical things: they have nothing to do with a particular 'religion'. The lesson is that to attain our higher potentiality, we are not to make religion the bridge between ourselves and the higher cosmic principles. In fact, sometimes it is important to discard religious beliefs. Because that can keep us restricted.

Great leadership is one where respect for values is recognized above all. Where your inner truth starts awakening, being activated to a degree where you can act with great faith: not faith based on what someone is telling you, but what you see with your own mystic eye. And so doing, transform yourself, thereby attaining a power to help transform things in the material world also.

Most of us live restricted to certain dimensions: we have the religious dimension, we have the political dimension, and so on. But truth is multi-dimensional. Truth is not something which can be contained within the pages of a book. It is all about vision. It is all about what the sages of India called Drishti, Darshana. The ability to see deeply into things. And it is this base of Drishti which Krishna is inculcating in Arjun. To make him realize his individual freedom and dignity as a spiritual being, and thereby act. What is important in the leaders of tomorrow is the need to enable people's feelings of dignity: this creates an egalitarian feel to the way their organization works. Where there is dignity of spiritual values, there comes about great power to work in tandem with each other. And to create something which is truly beyond definitions of 'us and them'.

The problem with religion is that it creates duality: we identify with *our* community or religion, and thereby become rather restricted or parochial in our view. But in an increasingly globalized world, we have to see that leadership becomes such that people can exist as a broader global community, without constantly being in state of tension with each other. And this begins with leaders understanding this within their own consciousness. And essentially the Bhagavad Gita is about *leadership consciousness*. The energy of the mind is to start turning to a deeper and more meditative state, for out of such a state comes really alert action: action which is non-tense and non-anxious, but has a deep quality of dynamism inherent in it. Therefore, what is really important is that you act out of such understanding.

We are taught throughout our education system, throughout our societal training, that respect for values and love for values are perhaps not as important as simply 'getting ahead'! But where will you go, where will you 'get ahead' without respect and love for values? If you don't have respect for values, you cannot expect respect to accrue to you from others. There will be awe maybe in the eyes of others, but true respect is gained by having a sensibility of respect for values. In fact, in the Mahabharat, when the great patriarch Bheeshma is dying on the bed of arrows, Krishna very directly tells Yudhishthira to go and consult him on what leadership means. Now, Yudhishthira is going to become the next king, the emperor of the land. He goes very humbly to Bheeshma, and the patriarch tells him that respect is to be earned in a manner which is beyond position. What he said is that a king is respected by his subjects, but a person of wisdom is respected by all! So that is the kind of leadership vision that the Mahabharat as a whole professes. That is real Dharma.

Hence, authentic leadership is all about transforming ourselves into a higher level of being. And when we transform ourselves into a higher level of being, we begin transforming things on the outer sphere. If we ourselves are not transformed, how can we begin transforming others to a degree where they become more effective? This is a fundamental message of the Gita.

A great leader gets his or her people to create useful things. To work with excellence and effectiveness. A great leader strives to create value. But all these goals are a product of our basic vision. And that vision is not necessarily an intellectual vision, but rather one which is shaped through spiritual and aesthetic clarity. Through a realization of higher principles, which the Gita condenses and exemplifies. Without those, we remain simply exhausted travellers on this journey of life.

So many leaders have come and gone without creating true value. If you want to create real value, have respect for life itself. Have respect for that which is truly valuable, and have respect for humanity. That does not mean you shirk from a fight, it does not mean that you stay away from fighting for what is right! In fact, that is what Krishna is encouraging Arjun to do. But in the end, what it really means is that even while you use your logic and reasoning, do not be dominated by the prison of thought. Intelligence comprises not only thought, but more importantly our spectrum of vision. And that vision is one which is to be born of empathy, clarity, deeper understanding. Then only does one become a person who is truly *responsible* in both the mystical and the material domains. And great leadership is all about being able to bear great responsibility.

'Maya' Means Thinking You Are the Centre of All Things

LESSON: The veil of cosmic illusion or 'Maya' makes one identify with one's personality, name, position of power, and so on. It takes one away from the root reality of self, that is comprised of pure consciousness and pure energy. Identify yourself more with consciousness and energy, and less with external and humanly created 'labels'. This lesson lets one ideate and act freely and vigorously, released from all limitations of material, mental, cultural, and emotional conditioning. The secret of cheerful success and dynamic leadership is in destroying the illusion of the 'I'. This creates fulfilment at every level of your being.

The greatest illusion or *maya* of mankind is that we are somehow the centre of the universe. Our whole view of the cosmos is related to ourselves. Think for a moment: even if mankind ceases to exist in the cosmos, the cosmos will still be there as it is, without any difference! So really, the whole idea of thinking that somehow we are central to the scheme of things or that we are very important in the scheme of things—even at a very material level (in our everyday work as leaders and so on)—is the biggest illusion. And Krishna very clearly demonstrates this to Arjun through his mystic teachings in the Gita.

Krishna hammers Arjun at a psycho-spiritual level into realizing that none of us as human beings really matter in a material way. We may have something material one moment, and we lose it the next moment. *Yet we do matter, profoundly, in a spiritual way!* And this is what Arjun realizes: that as a participant on the material field, he is perhaps not as important as he was thinking. What is important are the larger cosmic principles which Krishna represents. Sometimes leaders are so self-obsessed, that they place themselves as the centre of everything. In that way, leadership can be the most ego-nourishing exercise! The idea can prevail that it is the actions of the leader which determines things. This itself is a very unhealthy way to look at the subject of leadership. This needs to change, no matter how big a leader is. No matter if they are an Abraham Lincoln or a Steve Jobs in their respective fields.

The sense of self-obsession and self-importance is the most destructive force from the spiritual point of view because it misleads us into believing we are important. Ultimately, none of us are important as far as the cosmos goes. All that is important in us is how much we have been able to realize our cosmic connection in the inner world of ourselves. And through that realization, we are to act dynamically within the world, to an extent that the divine energy functions through us. To an extent that we feel the highest ecstasy and experience the greatest joy! And in the experiencing of this comes about the success and fulfilment of our life.

So, let us pay attention to the spiritual part. Else we remain in an illusion of our self-importance. After all, how important is a human being by himself: we all live just for a few decades, we all have little time! Our lives don't have much importance beyond a very limited circle of the human sphere. Rather, we can argue that mankind has done more harm than good on earth. If mankind becomes extinct on earth, maybe it's better for all the other species, for the flora and fauna!

Hence, ultimately we are not so important. And the beauty is, if you take away the sense of self-importance, then you find that something takes place within which is really mystical. Then you find that you are simply a small part of that vast life-energy which exists in the universe. And you function from that state! So whatever you do becomes an expansion of that life-energy. Whatever you do expands you, de-limiting you from self-imagined boundaries. Then do you go into the realm of the timeless, then do you go into the realm of the eternal. Otherwise you remain very limited in your scope of perception.

The idea of expansion itself liberates us at the mental and spiritual levels. Do not get trapped in the ultimate trap of leadership consciousness, which is the sense of self-importance. Rather, try and move into empathy. Because from empathy comes about a feeling of oneness with the greater aspect of existence. The relationship we have with the cosmos is ultimately the means of self-realization. So never forget that *that* is your authentic and original being. The rest of it is pure illusion, what has been called Maya.

Immerse yourself in the feeling that you are in a direct relationship with a higher power. And when you feel this arise in your being, then you come into a better relationship with all that exists in the material world. Eventually, all great leadership is about interpersonal relationships; but if your relationship with the vaster aspects of existence is strong, so too become your relationships in the material sphere. Because it is just a question of being empathetic and open. Krishna is just indicating that it is the obstinacy of Arjun's mind which is the only barrier which prevents him from realizing his higher nature. There is no other barrier. And the best way to destroy this barrier is to arouse his spiritual energy, because through the vibration of spiritual energy do we move towards a broader understanding of things.

It is very moving to hear the account of Arjun talking to Lord Krishna and saying how every hair on his body has stood up when he beholds the cosmic form of the Lord! How he is almost having goosebumps! How his heart is throbbing in trepidation. But it is this moment of transformation—because the individual is able to see beyond himself and into a higher reality—that is really the hallmark of any great leader. Of someone who expects to do something greater and more profound than others. Because only such people are able to transcend their normal limitations. And great leaders are those who can transcend the normal limitations of most people, accomplishing that which seems impossible to others.

For you to be a great leader, be fully prepared to go into challenges. Be fully prepared to go into dangerous situations, where you can even be shattered! Be prepared for real risk. Find courage from realizing wholeheartedly this one truth: that we are on earth to use the completeness of our spiritual energy into seeking the *higher* principle. Because that is actually the centre of existence, and not us. The word 'Krishna' itself means that which is at the centre of all things and is attracting all things. It is an apt metaphor for us to understand from the leadership success point of view.

Everything Goes Together: Life and Death, Success and Failure

LESSON: Krishna bridges the extremes and polar opposites of life. We are to understand not to be obsessive about any circumstance, emotion, thought, or feeling. Great leaders remember that in the midst of joy, sorrow can come. In the midst of prosperity and boom, doom and gloom can come with great speed. Alternately, during difficult times, a ray of hope can come and brighten all things. The idea is this: be alert to the opposite. Then you become better prepared as a leader and as an individual, ready for anything! Readiness and alertness of being are the hallmark of true success and great leadership.

Maturity *(paripakvata)* in leadership implies being able to understand the duality of all things. Material phenomena have two sides: where there is success, there is also failure, just as in the way that where there is life, there is also death. This is a very vital leadership lesson to understand: if you want to be mature in your leadership approach, don't obsess with success. Remember, the other side of the coin is failure. Don't obsess with life, because the other side of the coin is death. This is a subtle understanding. What Krishna is telling Arjun is not about success or victory, but it is *how* Arjun is to fight, how he is to live, which matters.

Concentrate on the quality itself, for that is the key. That is what creates maturity—and moments of true value—in your leadership. When you concentrate on the quality more than outcomes, then do you relax. If you are obsessed with what will follow—for example, if you're obsessed with death or the fear of death—you'll never be relaxed. You have to be a little aloof, detached from your own thoughts! As a leader, if you are obsessed with success only, then small failures can also break you, shatter you. Because you are not prepared for them. So Krishna is making Arjun's heart and mind such that no matter what the results of the battle, he is able to adapt. Adaptability implies maturity. Then one's whole life, one's whole existence, becomes very original in action. It becomes imbued with the energy of the *eternal* factor, the great factor behind all things. Of the *hidden hand* which shapes the world.

It is important to understand the duality of material phenomena, and concentrate on quality more than outcome. This is exceedingly important in a world where people are undergoing so many psychological problems: the pressure of work has led to increase in the rate of suicide, the rate of burnout and depression. What is the primary reason for this? It is because people have unrealistic hopes and expectations. They obsess with success, and are broken by even small failures! Therefore, it is important for us to inculcate an attitude which is resilient. A leader with a resilient mind—resilient to change, to failure, to disruption—is one who can go beyond the trivial and the unnecessary. And attain the true treasure, the true success of his being.

You will find the streak of adaptability and maturity in great leaders. Look at the world of business: Thomas Alva Edison (who has been an icon for so many entrepreneurs and innovators around the world) was well known for carrying on persisting even in the face of failure. For every success he had, he had a thousand failures! But in the end, what mattered were his successes. He did not allow the thought of failure to put him down. And that is why he emerged as a dynamic and exemplary leader in the world of technology and human progress. He introduced technology which improved the quality of life for billions.

So really, we have to be concerned with ourselves in

a manner where we are able to see that our minds do not get disturbed or distracted by fear of the negative factor. And the only way to do that is to understand the intrinsic two-sided nature of any phenomena: they are two sides of the same coin! Two aspects of the same effort.

It's not necessary that every effort has to lead to victory, it is not necessary that everything has to move towards an outcome which you thought would happen. The outcome is not the thing: it is the underlying unity of your heart and mind. It is your comprehensive being which should function in harmony, through understanding that all things are just possibilities, and not certainties. Else you can become neurotic; you can become somebody like Adolf Hitler in your mindset. Hitler refused to entertain the thought of failure! And so doing, took millions of people to misery and destruction.

In the political sphere it is extremely important that leaders maintain a healthy and mature outlook. Else they'll just be bad losers, bad sportsmen so to speak, and lead people to misery. Politics is a cycle: defeat and success come and go. In the world of sports, we respect those who are able to lose gracefully. It is not the victory on the court or the pitch which is all-important, but also what values you have played with. If you've been unethical—if you've cheated—there is ultimately no point in winning. Like in cricket, what the Chappell brothers did against

New Zealand during the 'underarm bowling episode' (they won, but were disgraced). So that cannot be called good leadership, even if the outcome is victory. But if you've done the right thing in the right manner—have not cheated, but have given your best—then you can be called a good sportsman. So in the same way, in the political sphere and in the societal sphere, a true statesman will always be one who emphasizes a different attitude: not one of dominating the enemy or opposition, but of being graceful where one needs to be. And ultimately gracefulness is what gives us inner fulfilment. If we are not graceful in our behaviour—if we behave like brazen and utterly egoistic leaders—then downfall is certain!

It is interesting to listen to what the entrepreneur Elon Musk said about Steve Jobs. He personally didn't like him too much: he found him rude and grating. And in a way he is right, because Jobs became very ruthless at a point. But eventually, his life was very productive. Later on in his life, he did soften his stand on things. For example, he welcomed his children back into his life. He thereby attained a deeper sense of fulfilment, because he perhaps realized that material success is not everything! Sometimes it is good to bow down to a higher principle: to care for others, to be compassionate.

Death comes to us all, and death is a great teacher. The Gita is essentially about how death itself can teach us to live lives of quality, how death can help us understand the vaster cosmic implications of the gift of life itself. And the Upanishads too stress upon the primacy of death as being the greatest teacher (the Katha Upanishad is all about death in the form of Yama, conversing with the young Nachiketa on all aspects of being). But essentially, it is about not groping in the darkness of a one-sided approach, and *opening one's eyes to the totality of things,* the totality of possibilities. An alert leader is one who is aware of the phenomenon of totality! They are never broken by anything untoward which may happen, because they are prepared for it somewhere in their heart and mind. The immature leader is never prepared for a negative outcome: the negative outcome disturbs and shatters him. Hence, such leaders do not attain an enduring positive attitude of leadership or a strong attitude of leadership.

Strength in leadership ability implies that you have to uncover those depths in yourself which can be completely receptive to whatever comes your way! No matter what the result or outcome.

CHAPTER-15

The Conqueror Must Be Free of the Feeling of Being a Conqueror (Vijeta)

LESSON: The only real 'victor' in life is the cosmic force, that which you may call Nature or the Divine. Krishna brings Arjun to a ground-level understanding of this through the display of His cosmic splendour. Man should never think himself to be invincible. Foolish pride always goes before a great fall. Be humble, gracious, dignified, and strong. These are key to one's leadership presence and central to the Gita's wisdom.

One of the principal understandings which Krishna is seeking to instil into Arjun is that even if he is the winner, the victor, or the conqueror, he must be free of the feeling of being so. The very idea that the individual is the conqueror *(vijeta),* is the whole problem.

History is witness to many leaders who have conquered great lands and won great victories. Yet their lives and totality of being have often been meaningless and destructive. Because the sense of being 'a conqueror' remained in their hearts and minds. And out of the sense of becoming a conqueror has come about immense cruelty, injustice, ego-trips. So what the Lord is teaching is that you must fight the fight, walk the path, because that is the Warrior's Way, yet never feel within yourself that you are the 'Conqueror'. Because only the Supreme is the Conqueror of all things. The only 'Kingdom' you can really conquer is your own Kingdom: within yourself. If you master your own inner kingdom then you become the real victor in life. And if you cannot master the inner kingdom within yourself, then you are just a beggar in life, no matter how great a leader or a king you are. Jesus also says, 'The kingdom of God is within you.' And this echoes what the Lord says in the Gita: that it is within you, but if the feeling of 'doer-ship' or the feeling of being egoically powerful exists within you, you are never able to conquer that kingdom. And what does conquering the kingdom mean? Conquering the inner kingdom means attaining more and more enlightened wisdom about your purpose in the world. About your Dharma, your duty, your divine calling, yourself.

The problem which has happened throughout history

is that most people who have been in positions of great power have not had the wisdom to go along with that power. And that has ultimately not only destroyed millions of other lives and damaged the earth, but it eventually also consumed the conquerors themselves, the kings themselves! There are very few exceptions: Emperor Ashoka the Great learnt that by conquering the kingdom of Kalinga he had not really 'conquered' at all. Rather, he had destroyed. It is only due to his spiritual realization—when he realized that the inner kingdom is the one worth conquering—that his life became meaningful. Then he became known as the 'Great'. Before that, he was never called Ashoka the Great. He became great only after he left this feeling of being the conqueror.

In fact, this feeling of being a conqueror is a common problem of powerful leaders. But what they don't realize is that it takes away their fundamental spiritual energy. What they also don't realize is that it takes away their ability to be discerning and wise in their thoughts or actions, in their choices. Ego always ends up making the wrong choices! And making the wrong choices is the most terrible thing a leader can do. The best thing a leader can do is make right choices, be a good decision-maker. And good decision-making only comes out of a real sense of Dharma and wisdom. Do not get clouded by the clouds of thought which continually remind you that you are the ultimate 'Conqueror': that is only going to take you into an ego trip! And not allow you to go into the greater sky of infinity which we are part and parcel of. Go into clarity of seeing things beyond the clouds of self-importance, and then you rise higher and higher. And out of this consciousness—of rising in your ability of perception—whatever comes will be good.

Wisdom always has a way of rewarding the person who has it. Of course it may seem sometimes that even people of wisdom are losing the battle, but eventually they are the ones who attain something much deeper. Because they have the eye of intuition. A person who is lost in a power trip loses their intuition. They lose what is really valuable, and identify themselves with the fruits of the victory. And the fruits of the victory are exactly what Krishna advises Arjun not to identify with! Because those are very small things, those do not really lead to contentment or fulfilment. They are the plastic flowers which cannot be a substitute for the sweet fruits of wisdom in the thing that's called the *kalpataru*: the metaphorical wish-fulfilling tree. What Krishna wants Arjun to do is to pluck the fruit. Each teaching of the Gita is like that sweet fruit. The warrior is meant to eat it. That fruit gives wisdom, that fruit gives nourishment. It nourishes one at the levels of complete mind-body-spirit. It enriches us and makes us braver in the physical sphere, and at the same time it makes us more alert in the mental sphere, giving us a deep contentment and realization in the spiritual sphere! Which is why the Gita has been called the most complete text in the world of spirituality and mysticism by several great people. Because it gives a body-blow to dogma, and defeats the idea that your happiness should be derived out of the position, the power, the wealth which you have. It cuts that root of misunderstanding and instead replaces it with something more real and meaningful, which cannot be taken away from you.

Power, position, wealth: all these come and go! The only thing which is eternal, permanent, and timeless is that which belongs to the higher sphere of consciousness. And the Gita is all about consciousness. If in your consciousness you are free of the ego of being the 'winner' of the battle, then only do you become *the real winner* of the battle. This is also a fundamental difference between the two brothers Arjun and Karna. Karna is often temperamental and egoistic, while Arjun does not have so much ego. He is much clearer and much more innocent in his thinking. And therefore, eventually the victory is his! Because the truth of the Supreme is always with the person who is devoid of the baggage of ego. With he who does not consider himself to be supreme just on the merits of his skills. It is not skills alone which lead to victory. This is a very, very important principle.

Some people always think that they are 'better' simply because they have a better set of skills. But in life also you would see that it is those with a deeper sense of stillness, calmness, and coolness of being who achieve all-round victory.

Being invested in a sense of importance when it comes to skills can be damaging. Unegoistic people are often more successful because they are able to do things in a much freer manner, not tied down by what others will think about them. The main problem with egoistic people—or with people who are conquerors, like great emperors and kings were in the past—is that they have a lot to lose! They are always insecure: what if their position gets lost or gets destroyed? So they're always insecure. They're always working out of a sense of dread and fear. And therefore, they commit wrong actions.

Leaders who do not carry the idea of identifying themselves with the position they are in, or the victory they have achieved in a battle, have nothing to lose. They look forward to things with a new eye, and so doing they become almost undefeatable. Because, how can you defeat a person who's already prepared to be defeated? In this very sense of vulnerability—in how they are able to free their mind and heart to function to a maximum degree—they become much surer about themselves. They become more relaxed in their own strength. They know their own power or personal power, and act out of that. And out of that not only does true victory come, but joy also follows as a natural consequence.

CHAPTER - 16

Never Think You Know Everything

LESSON: Keep evolving, keep moving on towards the brighter radiance of your being. Your focus on spiritual evolution will make you transcend and overcome all obstacles, all stumbling blocks. It is the secret of truly successful people and great leaders: they never stop learning and evolving, hence never get trapped in self-consciousness. Be light on the journey of life: look at it as a great adventure of the soul, during which it expands and evolves timelessly. And we are pure soul! Through this vision, all crisis situations can be looked at as mere chapters on the soul's adventure. Hence, challenges don't overwhelm you, but lead you instead to mind-body-soul progress.

Arjun had reached the ultimate peak of being a warrior *(yoddhha)*. He was considered the greatest warrior alive. The only person who could come close to his warrior abilities was Karna. But still, Arjun had to learn from the Lord the real secrets of warrior-hood. It was not about learning particular skills, but learning the real skill and real art of being a warrior. Of being the unattached warrior, the ultimate warrior, the one who did his duty or Dharma. This he had to learn from Lord Krishna. The lesson for leadership is that we are never to stop evolving, we are never to think that we know everything that is to be known. Because the moment we do that, we stop evolving and learning.

This is a common problem with leaders: once they attain a leadership position, they start thinking they know a lot. And thereby they stop experiencing the higher truth of leadership. Krishna takes Arjun by the hand and guides him unto the greatest secrets of leadership and warrior-ship: then only does he evolve. All that he has known in the past is dead. Now he has to go forth boldly into a new future, and do the battle with a new frame of mind.

So this going into every challenge and every situation with a fresh frame of mind is the real secret of evolved warrior-hood and evolved leadership. Krishna brings Arjun to a point of breaking him: He brings him to tears. He brings him to fear. He brings him to trembling. He brings him to see something higher. But yet all through these processes, evolution comes. Evolution is not an easy process: evolution requires you to lay down what you have known. To accept that you don't know everything. Only then will you truly evolve in consciousness. And that is what real liberation and fulfilment in life is, not just for leaders but for every human being.

Fundamentally, if you want to be an evolved leader and if you want to keep evolving higher, the thing is to not get stuck psycho-spiritually. Move on to the higher, move on to the more blissful, move on to the evolutionary path. And that is what Arjun does. Because he is an evolved person, he understands that he has to move forward without getting stuck in a feeling that he knows a lot or has achieved a lot. And he has the ultimate teacher, the ultimate master, who takes him beyond his past identity as a warrior and teaches him that he is to move on to a greater glory of being of consciousness. Then only will the true victory come to him.

That is the way of the genuine warrior and the genuine leader: for true victory, you have to move on. You have to burn the past. You have to move to a situation where there is no ego anymore. And the greatest ego in the world is the ego of saying 'I know!'. Nobody knows ultimate truths except the Supreme. The very idea of feeling 'I know' defeats the evolution of the human being.

There's a very interesting story in Greek traditions about how the Oracle of Delphi was asked who is the wisest man on earth. And she tells the questioners that it is Socrates. But when the people go to Socrates with this answer, he says, 'I don't know anything.' So they go back to the Oracle of Delphi, who is supposed to know inner and hidden things. And they tell her that Socrates says he knows nothing, so how could she have said that he's the wisest person? And she says yes, that is why she calls him the wisest person: because he *knows* he doesn't know everything! Others think they know everything. This is what makes Socrates wise.

So the dawning of wisdom and inner harmony, the dawning of inner rhythm, is a result of saying 'I don't know everything'. Of accepting it in the very core of your bones! Then do you move on to something higher. Otherwise you become stuck. You're a lake, stagnant— you don't become a river which flows into the ocean. And every being has to evolve into flowing into the ocean of existence. Move on!

In the Upanishads it is said, '*Charaiveti, Charaiveti!*': 'Move on, keep moving on.' And this is exactly what the Buddha also said. You have to move on from what you have known. You have to move on from that which you think is your position, your power. Don't get entangled or bound. If you get entangled in it, there is absolutely no chance that you will reach towards your higher nature.

There is no stop to evolution. It is a continuous process. Just because you have attained a particular position—you may have become the CEO, you may have become the president, you may have become the head of an organization or a nation—does not mean that you stop learning. Let all these thoughts disappear, just as all these thoughts disappeared from Arjun's mind. And through that, he became much more available to the infinity of truth. As the result of all this, he became a better warrior. Even the way he fought changed. Because now he fought with a psychological and spiritual freedom, without any mental disturbance. He became so dynamic and feared as a warrior—more than ever—and unstoppable.

Hence, to become unstoppable and unlimited as an individual it is very important that you come out of the dream and the misunderstanding that you know a lot. Only when you come out of the dream can you fly higher into the sky of achievement. People get bound down by their own sense of ego and ambition. Ambition should not be about achieving a certain position. It should be about evolving enough so that the position comes on its own. It is not a question of cunning; it is not a question of being very clever. That is a very narrow-minded way. The real way is to move towards that which is the greatest part of you, that which is the ultimate force which resides within you. Which is the microcosmic reflection of the cosmos itself.

The supreme life is a journey towards the Supreme, in our own individual ways. If you are a leader, you can also take your people and your team onto this unlimited path of self-actualization. But don't stop after you've climbed the first mountain. Move on! There's another Mount Everest to climb. And in the world of consciousness, in the world of evolution, there is no such thing as the highest peak! The peaks are higher and higher! It just requires you to first accept that you don't know too much, and with that humility go into things. Be ready to learn, and then what happens is you automatically develop the power for higher fulfilment in every manner: material, psychological, spiritual.

Life is a journey of awakening to greater consciousness. And leadership should also be a journey of awakening to this higher consciousness. Because only then can you experience the totality of yourself, of your self-potential. Otherwise your potential gets blocked by your very inability to see beyond your power and position. Most leaders cannot see that sometimes their position and power is what restricts them. They make that the basis of everything. And thereby, they become burdened by that power and position. It becomes a poison instead of becoming a nectar. A real leader has the ability to move on!

In history, a good example of a great leader is Chandragupta Maurya. Even at the height of his name, fame, and power as the emperor of the great Magadh kingdom, he moved on. While he was just in his early forties, he became a monk. The idea is not that we become monks; the idea is not that we renounce the whole idea of getting stuck with what we know and what we have. It is that willingness of creating a higher goal, whatever it may be. For one person it may be becoming spiritual, but for another person it may be just the ability to have more insight into one's subject.

Whether one is a businessman, a statesman, an entrepreneur, a scientist, a musician, an artist, a political leader, or anything else, it should be a process of knowing and evolving into one's subject more deeply. If an artist starts thinking that the music he created yesterday was the greatest ever, then he cannot evolve from that point. Mozart or Beethoven didn't restrict themselves by that feeling. They moved on. Similarly, a great scientist has an open mind. This openness of mind is what creates an Albert Einstein or a Stephen Hawking. The courage to say 'I don't know everything', and to be open to truth is the key. For a person of science that truth could be scientific, for a spiritual seeker it could be the spirit—the mystical search for truth, and so on.

For an entrepreneur, it could be evolving from

one challenge after the other. Which is why a serial entrepreneur like Elon Musk is so respected: because he doesn't stop. He keeps trying to evolve new solutions for humanity. Even Thomas Edison was like that: one challenge after the other. The pursuit of excellence and success requires us to be ready to evolve. This is a basic foundational principle for all things, including leadership.

The Gita Proves that Wisdom Can Dawn Anywhere

LESSON: The beauty of Krishna's Gita is its profoundly soulful vision that real transformation is instantaneous and can happen anywhere! In fact, it happens more quickly when we are faced with challenges. This is exactly what happens to Arjun, who is upon the theatre of war, on the brink of battle! Leaders would do well to remember this: turn all crises into transformative moments. This is the very heart, the very essence of the Bhagavad Gita.

One of the most fascinating things about the Gita is that it is conveyed on the field of battle *(ranbhumi)*, in the midst of war. This is very important to understand: that in any situation— whether we are in any crisis or circumstance—

the voice of supreme wisdom is available to us. Just as Krishna becomes available to Arjun.

Mystical knowledge and spiritual realization is not something we have to go into a monastery for. It is available in the midst of all our actions, no matter whether we are leading in a battle or in any other situation in life, amidst work of any kind.

Spiritual realizations—those of bliss, compassion, love, and passion for what we do—can possibly happen even in the middle of crisis situations. And a battle is an ultimate crisis situation. It is a crisis reaching crescendo; it is a pivotal point for leadership decision-making. But even there, inward bliss can be found. Great fulfilment can be found.

So through the Gita we realize that no matter what we are doing—we could be leading a business organization, we could be facing a challenge in a situation at work, we could be in the midst of solving a crisis or firefighting a circumstance—even there, and in fact there most of all, the Supreme is knocking at our door. Wisdom is knocking at our door. It only requires us to be awake to the possibility of wisdom. That is the essential thing. Then we will find that no matter in what activity we are occupied, we can still find the meditative, balanced, contemplative, dynamic state of heart and mind to function.

This is what makes the Gita very unique, and this is

what makes it perhaps the most practical spiritual text as well as the vastest. Because it does not tell us that we have to run away from our work or our duty. But rather tells us the opposite: that in the midst of duty can be found the highest service and the highest religion, the highest spirituality! All else will follow from there.

Hence, you are to make your very work imbued with your mystical and spiritual consciousness. And if you can do that in the midst of work, then you are truly worthy of having a blissful life. It is very easy to run away from your work and find a place for meditation, prayer, or worship. But if you can bring spiritual awareness into your work, then you go beyond all challenges. You transcend challenges and thereby find the courage and wisdom to lead well, to act properly as a leader.

Try it in your own life: in the midst of whatever leadership role or work you are in, just remind yourself of that suppressed part of you which can be made available to a higher wisdom. If you are in a situation which is very explosive at the material level, bring a spiritual calmness to it. Bring the quality of spiritual equipoise and equanimity to the most crisis-bound situations. And then you will find your leadership ability going up to a very high degree. If you can act with deep calmness during crisis situations, think about the kind of respect your team will have for you. This is where the Gita is supreme in its ability to cleanse us and to take us to our authentic being. To create a catharsis within us. And all this is to happen very spontaneously.

The only spirituality which is worth anything is that of deep awareness in the midst of all activity. And that is exactly what Krishna is teaching Arjun. Just remember that beyond the canvas of the mind is the essence of wisdom. Beyond the canvas of all activity is the Supreme Energy which powers it all. And what you must do is remember it, and contact it in those moments of life when you most need it. Yet the problem is, most people forget to tap into their own reservoirs of wisdom. When they're dealing with their teams, clients, or opponents, they often lose themselves: they get angry, they allow like or dislike, jealousy, or comparison to come in. But if during these interactions and these moments you can remember yourself as being one with the supreme wisdom which exists in the cosmos, then your action starts getting more authentic, more deeply rooted and energetic. That is the way of the warrior: calm amidst crisis, fearlessness in the face of death, spiritual remembrance in the face of injury.

Not only in India has this 'Warrior Code' been prevalent, but it has been emulated by the samurai warriors of Japan. Especially the spiritual values which talk about personal leadership and truly successful living.

CHAPTER - 1 8

Prepare to Fight

LESSON: The principle of 'fight'—of never running away from challenges—is the soul of the Gita. It is also the key to real success and great leadership. Confrontation leads to the upsurge and expression of sheer guts. And guts are the most important thing needed by anybody seeking true success, and most of all by a leader. Without real guts, there is neither true material success nor spiritual fulfilment. Look all problems in the eye, direct! This awakens your highest human potential. Then even the divine element is compelled to strengthen you further.

It is a sad reality of human history that some of the most awakened and peaceful souls have had to endure terrible persecution or violence.

Whether in the East or the West, the story is the same: the powerful are always persecuting those who they think are a threat. The powerful are always meting out injustice to those who are the voice of consciousness. Countless have been the persecutions, including Socrates in Greece and Jesus Christ in the Middle East. But Krishna is telling Arjun that the person who is really awake is somebody who is willing to fight for the right thing! He tells him to pick up his bow and fight, not just endure the injustice. If the cause is worth fighting for, fight we must! That is the warrior's way, the true leader's way.

Why is this important? You would think the mystical and spiritual path would profess only peace. But that is not the case. We must do that which is just. As long as we are on the side of justice, as long as we are on the side where we are defending the freedom of choice and the freedom of people, we must learn how to fight. This has nothing to do with terrorism or unjust violence, because terrorism is an act where you inflict injury upon innocent people. But this is simply an act where you meet the enemy head-on, in a very noble way. And both sides agree to certain rules about how to fight. It is very surprising that in the Mahabharat there are depictions of warriors from both camps visiting each other after battle hours, in a friendly way: in fact, when the Pandavs were not succeeding in killing Bhishma, they themselves went to him in the Kaurav camp and asked his advice about how he can be defeated. So, as long as the engagement is fair, and not born out of malice or ill-will, then one must prepare to fight.

This is a hallmark throughout the Mahabharat and throughout the Gita: don't run away from any fight. If you do that, you are not really awake to moral justice. Be on the side of truth, and victory is yours. And how do we decide what is truth? You can do that only when you come to a spiritual realization that what you are doing on the battlefield is worth it, because through the act of battle you are actually saving millions of others from misery (if injustice wins). Had the Kauravs and Duryodhan won the battle, it would have meant subjecting the innocent citizens of the land to great injustice, to the wrong kind of leadership, to the egoic kind of leadership which people such as Duryodhan and his brothers were prime examples of. If you do something which empowers the wrong person or the wrong set of people, then you are not a good leader. This is exactly the kind of reasoning that the great scientist J Robert Oppenheimer—who initiated the Manhattan Project, which went on to make the atomic bomb—relied on. In fact, on his own he had learned Sanskrit and read the Bhagavad Gita multiple times while at Harvard University. And he came to the conclusion that he has to utilize his talents and his intelligence to fight on the side of right, which he realized was for the Allies against the Germans and Japanese. The Axis powers were relentless in their war effort, and ultimately the atomic bomb was born. And while it is deeply unfortunate that millions died as a result of this act, Oppenheimer himself quoted the Gita during the test run of the bomb. After it had exploded, he quoted Krishna's words 'And I am become death, the destroyer of all worlds.' It is not a question about whether we believe the atom bomb to be a creation of good or evil. It in fact started a nuclear age which has led to a lot of problems and uncertainty in the world of today. But what is really important is that sometimes when the opposition is relentless, it is imperative for the warriors who follow the code of justice and rightfulness to stand up and fight. Of course for the atom bomb the problem which happened was the Japanese were simply refusing to surrender, and it became a war which was dragging on, killing millions more.

In my personal opinion, the way Oppenheimer interpreted the Gita to justify his creation of the atom bomb was fundamentally wrong. In fact, in his later years he became the biggest proponent of the anti-nuclear stand. He refused to have anything to do with the more powerful hydrogen bomb which was being developed. He became an absolute objector to the whole idea of nuclear weapons, because he realized that while Krishna was talking about personal courage in one-to-one combat, creating mass destruction was in fact a cowardly way. It is not the way of true warriors. At the time of Kurukshetra, when Krishna was exhorting Arjun to not shy away from his own integrity as a warrior, it was about being there and doing the fighting personally, against other warriors, courageously. Not sitting somewhere in the background and pressing a button, and in the process killing millions of innocent people. So while Oppenheimer's understanding of the Gita was eventually limited, and something he felt remorseful for his whole life, it does not mean that Krishna's message is limited. His message is for us at an individual level, and it is up to us to awaken our consciousness, to perceive the truth for our own interpretation. But the interpretation should not be one which takes us onto a path of mass destruction or of harming society in any way. In fact, just the opposite is true: the really noble warrior or leader always helps society. And that is what Krishna is exhorting Arjun to do.

What Krishna is telling Arjun is that there will never be peace if he does not fight the Kauravs. A Kaurav victory will not lead to peace. It will lead only to further conflict, further destruction, further war, because the Kaurav mind is war-oriented. And that is what happened with Japan during World War II: they had become so martial-oriented that they were simply not prepared to accept defeat! So it was just prolonging the misery more and more. Krishna tells Arjun, very subtly, that the essence of what he is implying is that if the fight is not taken to the fullest, then the question of peace will not arise. Sometimes, to achieve a higher end we have to fight. And this is an enduring lesson for leaders of all kinds: no matter what leadership position you are in.

There are some actions which are tough, there are some decisions which are tough, but they have to be taken! It may cause some momentary unhappiness, but as long as it leads to peace in the larger sphere, as long as it leads to a cessation of injustice against a relentless enemy or circumstance, we cannot shirk from the fight. Sometimes through friction and conflict comes about something new. A fresh start. Even if you look at the cosmos, it is through the friction and clash of opposites that universal creativity happens. So the concept of clash is not one that we ought to insulate ourselves from: in fact, it can lead to great creativity if applied correctly, for good causes.

Successful leaders are therefore prepared to go into clash. They do not wear a mask or try to act very compassionate when they do not really mean it. They are always endeavouring to make the hard decisions, but the important thing is that they do it with a feeling of goodness in their heart. It is not to be done out of malice. Leaders who are sometimes of an argumentative nature in the workspace are not necessarily the bad ones, because often creative team energy is born only through conflict and clash.

Flow into Totality

LESSON: The one thing that marks both great mystics and great leaders is vast and insightful vision. Spiritual capacity and leadership capacity are both dependant on that. Krishna's effort is to make Arjun have deep insight into, and flow with, the hidden mystic factor that He represents. Our vision becomes deep through having wonder for the cosmic life-force that sustains all things. Wonder and an attitude of gratitude open up our vision. They create a holistic worldview, making us acknowledge that ultimately it is the cosmic 'doer' who is acting through us. Through this holistic approach, one is able to act effortlessly, without worrying or doubting too much. Broadness of vision is an enabler of noble things: it allows us to excel as human beings and as leaders.

What is really remarkable about Krishna's life as evidenced in the Mahabharat is that only very few people knew his larger universal reality while he was in this particular avatar. Even his closest friend and ally, Arjun, did not see the wholeness or totality of cosmic consciousness which Krishna represented, before the episode of the Bhagavad Gita. What this fundamentally tells us is that even the wisest people in the land who existed during Krishna's human avatar, could not see the truth. Even they were conditioned and crippled in mind by society's conditionings, of various sorts: religious, ideological, political, and so on. And they could only see what this conditioning allowed them to see. So the learning is that most people can see through a very narrow keyhole: most people see through a tunnel vision; they miss the holistic totality of existence. But a real leader is one who grasps the spiritual totality of what is there, to a much greater degree than others. It is not a question of experience. If it were a question of experience, then all the sages who were alive during Krishna's time would have recognized him. But they did not! All the great meditators would have recognized him for what He was, but they did not.

It is the relatively inexperienced person in spirituality (Arjun) who is given the 'eyes' to recognize Krishna's truth. Arjun sees and recognizes Krishna for who He is, by Krishna's grace. Arjun is truly regretful and remorseful that he did not know Him for being this totality of universal consciousness earlier. He asks Krishna his forgiveness, saying that he thought He was just a friend and ally. The most intriguing part is that Krishna probably spent maximum time—amongst His friends—with Arjun, and also because they were related by marriage (Arjun was married to Krishna's sister Subhadra). So what this is telling us is that even when the Infinite is close to us, we are unable sometimes to recognize its subtlety. Even though the infinite power of the cosmic catalyst is right next to us, we are not seeing the truth of it. But those who can see the truth of it are those who can flow into totality: they meet with the highest potentiality of themselves. They become richer within themselves. And they become more capable of creating abundance and affluence outside themselves, because their energy multiplies. They become people who transcend ordinary energy and tap into the infinite energy which they recognize. Their lives become spontaneously filled with all the colours of the Infinite, and this shows in whatever they do. This shows in their inner wisdom. This shows in their 'inner eye'. They not only transform themselves, but also acquire the ability to transform others. And that is what a leader must do.

A great leader is a transformer of people. But first, the transformation has to happen within. And that transformation happens only when you yourself flow into totality, when you recognize that the infinite is always with you. The infinite power walks with you. You just have to recognize it. Through this recognition comes about a direct and heart-to-heart communication with a greater power—the total power—which drives existence. And then you become more deeply successful in your life, because knowing this greater power is ultimate success. Helping communicate this vaster power's work through your mind-body complex is the greatest ecstasy in life. We all have an opportunity to work 'God's work', so to speak: to make the earth a better place through our actions. To make our immediate environment better through our thought impulses and actions. But it only has true and abiding meaning if we feel total from within. If we feel that concentrated energy of the higher principle of life working through us.

Never feel alone, never feel that you are not complete. Completeness is just a capacity to see the totality which is with you always. And this totality of a higher power is with everyone. Some people recognize it, and express it through the actions of their lives. And some people are too caught up in the narrow conditioning of society, of religion, of politics, and so on. And then life is not truly successful: no matter what position you achieve, no matter what status you achieve.

A person who begins tapping into totality, recognizing

it, takes a great jump, a great leap into living life with an immense dynamism. And this shows in their very being, this shows in their very essence. Such a person becomes charismatic because fear vanishes. And when fear vanishes, one spontaneously becomes capable of leading people into good situations. Ultimately, both the leader and the followers are in the same divine game: the rules of which have been set by the supreme power, the cosmic power. The universe has just placed us in different circumstances. But it is up to us to recognize that we are to play a functional part in it with the totality of our energy. And the only way we can do so is by transforming our life patterns, through flowing with this totality and feeling that its presence is luminously with us. If only we choose to recognize it.

Knowing this principle of harnessing and flowing with totality is to become relaxed. Knowing it is to activate the deeper portions of yourself. And if you activate the deepest portion of yourselves, you act with wisdom. You act with both heart and head, in balance. The problem with a lot of people is that while they are skilful, there is something in the heart which is blocked: they're not able to release the full extent of their joy and ecstasy into their work. They hold something back, blocked within the heart centre. And the primary reason is that they live through conditioning: they look at reality through very narrow slits. They cannot grasp that the heart can be filled with a passion and an ecstasy, provided it is available to the universal ecstasy.

The universal force is with us every moment. Connect with it more consciously. In fact, you are no different from the universal force: if you are a drop of water, the universal force is the sea. Become one with it, feel one with it. And then you find that you can effortlessly go into all situations. Your mindset becomes that of a fearless and bold leader. And if your mindset is in a fearless leadership state, then nothing can stop you! No amount of conditioning can stop you. It all begins with allowing your individuality to flow into totality. That is the concept of real spiritual progress. But it also leads to progress in every sphere of life, including leadership in the material world. It is a foundational principle.

CHAPTER-20

Beyond Morality
Lies Freedom

LESSON: Krishna is not a moralist, but a universalist. He accepts all things including the weaknesses of his disciple Arjun. That is what makes Krishna and the Bhagavad Gita sublime. They have a grounded practicality, while taking us on a flight to the highest spiritual truth at the same time! That is the power of the Gita: it gives us tremendous freedom and never insists on any narrow moral code, as 'religious' scriptures usually do. In fact, great leaders too do not judge people narrowly through any limiting sense of morality. They encourage freedom of being, and that leads to great results. Openness is a hallmark of good leadership, and this can be evidenced in the 'out-of-the-box' thinking that good leaders encourage. Effective leadership means focussed yet open leadership, where

people are free to innovate and question. The success of this leadership style is evident at several technology companies. It is a broad principle that works in all spheres: business, art, science, and so on. Echoing the generous broadness of the Gita, generous leadership does not believe in dogma.

Several commentators in the past have called the Gita a moral compass for creating character. But in fact the Gita in its deeper essence deals not so much with a person's moral character, but with spiritual understanding that goes beyond any sort of morality. Perhaps the moral thing for the Master to do would be to ask his disciple to stop fighting, and to take a non-violent stance. But Krishna does the completely opposite thing: he advises Arjun to pick up his bow and fight. Not to be non-violent, but to jump into warfare if the cause of justice and of spiritual freedom is to be served. So it is about spiritual freedom, it is about unchaining Arjun from the sense of absolute right or absolute wrong.

Simple moral lessons deal with absolute right and wrong. But when it comes to deep esoteric texts like the Gita, you have to deal with contradictions. Hence, even while being a spiritual text, the Gita professes totality of action on the battlefield for the warrior. Because that is what his essential duty is in that moment. And that is what serves the cause of justice in the moment. This kind of teaching is easily misinterpreted. In fact, the Gita has been misinterpreted for all sorts of political or violent justifications. But essentially, it is all about being able to look past the illusory morality of so-called religion. And to attain a state of such utter freedom of mind and spirit, that one goes with deep compassion and a deep coolness of being even into the midst of warfare.

Arjun tells Krishna that his actions will lead to much bloodshed, but Krishna tells Arjun that even if the actions lead to bloodshed, it is a question of whether the actions are essential. Of whether the actions will bring about a real justice and a shower of freedom upon those who need it. So in that way, the Gita is about a deeper sort of 'meditation': it is about being meditative even in the midst of the battlefield. Meditation is the feeling of inward freedom. Meditation is the feeling of going beyond ordinary right and wrong. And of allowing the deeper vibrations of life to function through you. These vibrations being those of gratitude, compassion, love, and so on. Hence it is the *quality* of action which Arjun brings about, which is going to be the important thing. Not just the action itself. Sometimes the action is only an expression of something deeper. And if at the depth truth is served, then we are to look at the greater implications of the action which is being performed. Harshness has its own place, discipline has its own place, celebration of life has its own place: they are all relative to time and place.

Hence, the Gita is to be looked at in transcendental terms. As a text which takes away the warrior from the imprisonment of 'morality' and instead towards the sky of spiritual freedom. Be a warrior, yet be happy! This is what Krishna tells Arjun in essence. Be a warrior, and do not postpone that which needs to be done. Delight in the energy which the divine has imbued you with! Utilize that energy to maximum effect on the material sphere also. The material sphere is like the wave of the ocean: in itself it is nothing; it is only an expression of the depth of the ocean. It is actually only the outer face of a deeper dimension, and it is the *inner dimension* which the Gita is concerned with: the innermost being of Arjun, the innermost being of life itself, the innermost being of the meditative consciousness that is the building block of the entire universe.

We are to understand and imbibe the truth that our own minds are *unaware of who we really are*. Our minds forget that we are part of the cosmic ocean itself. We forget that we are of the same consciousness as the deepest depths of the cosmic ocean of consciousness. And it's identifying with the deepest depths of existence itself that the Gita is concerned with. In that way, it makes you see that you are a part of that ultimate reality which constitutes everything and is the building block of everything. Seeing this reality, there comes about a great release of your own innate energy, of your own innate potential, your own innate power. And that is the beginning of all successful journeys in life.

Fill the Emptiness within Yourself

LESSON: The most fulfilling things in life are intangible: gratefulness, compassion, devotion, wonder, quietness, meditativeness. Fill your life and leadership roles with these qualities, and you will move towards spontaneous and natural success.

The basic feeling that Arjun is experiencing is that of an emptiness of his heart. And the essential message of Krishna to Arjun is to fill that emptiness of the heart with the divine message *(divyasandesh)*. So spirituality is in the end a filling of the emptiness of life; it is a way of giving passion and meaning to life. It is a way of creating a blossoming of your very being. And of opening the doors of your perception to a reality which is of the meditative dimension.

The thing about life is that you can make all kinds of effort, but if your basic emptiness is not illumined by the light of the divine element, then what happens is the whole of life feels like a striving. It feels like a struggle. There is no feeling of fulfilment in the moment. There is only a feeling of wanting and craving more and more things.

So, the essential message of the Gita is to give us a glimpse into the very nature of the divine element. It is through Krishna deciding that the moment is right for Arjun to understand that it is not enough to be obsessed by the material factor of life. Arjun is in a state of deep worry, and his worry has become a very vicious psychosis within his being. It has paralyzed him; it has given him fear. In that way, Arjun is a metaphor for what we each are undergoing: we are all worried about things, we are all worried about being able to cope with things in the future. In that way, we become very confused within ourselves. We become very obsessed with our own anxieties. And we cannot grow much in the spiritual dimension. We become empty and devoid of the spiritual dimension. But what Krishna is saying is not to be self-centred, to not look at himself as a creature who has to act for a material goal. In fact, He tells Arjun that the material goal is not so relevant. The body may cease to exist in the course of the war, but what is really important is that Arjun comes to realize the truth of being. And realizing the truth of being is the essential step.

The Bhagavad Gita contains an essential message about how to fill the emptiness in our lives. What it indicates is that real happiness comes when you are least expecting it: happiness does not come out of material reward, but happens in those moments where you feel alive and contented with existence itself. So real contentment is essentially about feeling at peace with the world. And that is the contradiction of the way of the warrior. It looks like the way of the warrior is violent and aggressive, but really it is about feeling deep peace in the midst of violence and aggression. And that is why Krishna's message to Arjun is eternal. This peace cannot be purchased in the material world. This peace cannot be acquired by the mind. This peace is essentially about feeling the heartbeat of existence within your own heart, and merging with it. That is the inscrutable and mysterious message of the Bhagavad Gita.

So, it is about encountering and imbibing all that is truly meaningful in life. Not about intellectual activity or mental activity, but rather about the courage within the heart to know that wherever we are led in life, we are to go there with a sense of bravery. We are to go there with a sense of totality. Then nothing can break us. Then the very phenomenon of death becomes blunted. And this is the most wonderful feeling, because it fills the emptiness and replaces it with such a fullness of contentment, that it seems even if death comes, the warrior is ready to go against all odds!

It is not a question of feeling superior to the enemy. And that is what Krishna tells Arjun: it is not about creating a superiority complex or an aggressive complex. But it is about creating a great revolution of awareness within the heart. It is about having reverence for life and existence itself. But part of that reverence implies feeling the divine dimension even in the midst of battle, even in the midst of clash with others. The traditional way of religious morality is to avoid violence, is to avoid clash. But sometimes that becomes just an excuse for cowardice.

The warrior's way is the extraordinary way, because it professes your reliance upon yourself and stresses that the real need which has to be fulfilled within us is that of the human spirit. And that which fulfils the human spirit is really not material things, because they are less relevant and blunt when it comes to evolution of the spiritual dimension. Rather, having a passionate concern for the non-mechanical and non-material aspects of existence is the real mystical knowing. Knowing that whatever happens is good, knowing that you are to be rooted in the present moment, knowing that it is about your own inner experiences. And transferring these experiences to others in a positive manner. Knowing that you must have clarity in your mind; knowing that you must have balance! Because when these things are attained, then does grace descend upon us. And when grace descends upon us, we feel in no way empty. Rather we feel blessed, we feel quality of life, we feel integrated within our souls. And feeling integrated within our souls is what creates the real revolution in living. Because then you are not uncomfortable with yourself: you accept yourself, and you crystallize a great strength within your being. Out of this strength comes great success in whatever you touch.

Essentially, living is all about a proficiency in the mystic dimension and the meditative dimension. If that is solid, all good things follow: be it at the level of the material sphere, the mental plane, and so on. The main problem in human society is the psychological one: people have all sorts of negative beliefs which collectively create a very negative impact on the social environment, the ecology, and so on. It all begins with the psychology of our being. And the psychology which the Bhagavad Gita professes is one of seeking that which is truly fulfilling. It is essentially that silent aspect of being which allows us to feel still and contented within our own hearts, and experience the totality of ourselves. That is Grace, and that is the situation which the warrior looks forward to creating within himself or herself.

CHAPTER-22

It's All about Courage

LESSON: There is a hidden reserve of courage within you. Tap into it! The only difference between the 'hopeless' Arjun and the 'courageous' Arjun is the ability to move past anxious and doubting thoughts. Never think you are weak: you have a universe of courage within you. That is the real faith which the Gita professes. Always remember this principle. It is the most powerful lesson for tough times and difficult situations.

The Gita is all about courage. It says that to live courageously is the only way to live. And what is really required to become courageous, is mentally unburdening oneself of all factors that prevent dynamism!

In other words, leave aside your burdens like you would dust off dirt on your clothes. Move ahead dynamically! That is Krishna's divine message to Arjun. It is all about being fresh in your approach to life. About being adventurous, and not to look for security in life. In fact, life itself cannot be guaranteed by any measure. We live in a very precarious existence. Dynamic living means the ability to flow on, to move on. And in that very movement comes about the happiness of the human spirit.

The Gita teaches that great joy and great peace cannot come about by being stagnant. They always come about by the ecstasy of participating in whatever circumstances life presents us with. So the way to the divine, the way to God, the way to Higher Being, is always through the doorway of movement of spirit. In a manner where you are completely spontaneous. In a manner where you are completely open to whatever is presented to you as a human being. You are to have a relaxed attitude about things, to not get stuck by fear. And not getting stuck by fear is essentially what real bravery in life is all about.

These principles apply to every situation in life. Be that of our relationships—we are always insecure about whether a person will stay with us or not. Be it about a job—being insecure about whether we will be retained by the company tomorrow or not. Be it about our health—

whether we will survive healthily to a good old age. All these fears make man retarded in the spiritual sphere as well as the material sphere. And before you know it, life has been destroyed by this fear. To live in fear is the only betrayal of the divine.

The taste of the divine lies in fearlessness. This is what Krishna is trying to remind Arjun again and again. Because only through such fearlessness and courage does the spirit find bliss. And Krishna also shows Arjun that there is nothing to fear because Arjun is not alone! The Divine Energy which is perfectly beautiful is always with Arjun. He just has to spontaneously realize it in that very moment.

Through this stance of understanding—that one is not alone—one shrugs off confusion. One shrugs off worry, and therefore does not become too tense, does not keep moving in the same rut of one's old fears. But is able to come out of this rut with a great deal of dynamic energy, and thereby blossoms into what one truly is, to what is one's true potential. To fulfil oneself.

Human existence is often seen to be a state where one is continually frightened by outside goals and outside pressures. But real spontaneity begins with the realization that ultimately all wisdom is in becoming almost as if one is a child. Where one has a spiritually adventurous nature. An infant has so much courage to explore the new, such curiosity and wonder towards the new, such disconnectedness with the past and a fresh approach towards life. And that is what Krishna is teaching Arjun: have such a fresh approach towards the circumstances that are facing you that you are not bound up in fear.

In a modern context this is very important. Because we live in a very uncertain world, where everything can be interrupted by new developments and new happenings. In the world of work, in the world of business, disruption has become the norm. In ecological and environmental terms, we are facing more and more situations like floods and other natural calamities such as earthquakes and so on. Everything is in a flux, everything is uncertain. But in the midst of uncertainty, it is the power of stillness which allows us to explore the possibilities of our own potential. It is the power of being alertly meditative that is at the very foundation and basis of the mystic attitude. And this is what leads to an inner affluence of being, an inner affluence of understanding. And through this inner affluence of understanding comes about an unshakable courage, which in the end is the foundation of all good things that we do in life.

CHAPTER-23

Psychological Health
through Spirituality

LESSON: The Gita is not just a spiritual text but a textbook for the highest psychological well-being. And psychological well-being is indeed the key to true success and great leadership. Destructive leaders throughout history have been those who suffered psychological disorders: megalomania, inferiority or superiority complexes, and so on. Krishna is reminding Arjun to have no complexes at all: Arjun is feeling weak and inferior, and Krishna pulls him out of that mental abyss. Mental health for warriors and for leaders is the most important thing: the Gita effortlessly bridges the gap between the deepest psychological insights and the highest mystical truths. In that way, it is timeless: thousands of years ahead of modern psychology and psychotherapy!

The Bhagavad Gita is a coming back to psychological sanity *(maansik swaasthya)*. The whole text is about the human being's ability to see the beauty and joy of living productively, in a life-affirmative way. This itself brings about a great correction in the psychological problems which face humankind.

In its essence, the Gita is simple. But what it teaches is very profound. That though it is easy to fight in a state of psychological disturbance or in a state of psychological insanity, the real warrior is one who can fight and who can win against all odds through maintaining the stability of psychological sanity. So really it is about bringing the qualities of devotion, of trust, of positive imagination into whatever challenges we are faced with on the battlefield of life.

Krishna's ultimate message to the warrior prince Arjun is to understand that he is not to continue with the psychological disturbance which he is in, but rather is to look at a more enlightened manner of evolving within himself. Of creating that inner state of sanity which will win him not only self-respect, but respect within the world. And place him on a higher pedestal as far as his reputation and success as a warrior goes. So it is both an inward as well as an outward lesson for successful living. Inwardly, it teaches us about psychology and spirituality, and outwardly teaches us about how to create a position of respect within the world—by not postponing that which is essential and which needs to be done! Arjun is trying to escape and is trying to postpone the challenge which he is faced with, which is war with his cousins. But Krishna brings him back to reality again and again, and tells him to be humble about his duty at hand. He tells him that it is not about seeking power through fighting, but it is through fighting in a meditative state that Arjun will attain all that needs to be attained by the true warrior amongst men.

So in other words, the speciality of the Gita is that it tells us to shed the walls of limiting thoughts which have surrounded us from all sides. And only by shedding those walls do we begin evolving in both the spiritual and the material spheres of life. Psychological illness is a product of surrounding our mind on all sides with imagined thought processes and imagined fears. The moment you are ready to drop these walls of anxiety and fear intensely and totally, you come to a situation where you become deeply contented and blissful within. You come to a situation where you function out of a sense of wholeness and happiness. And when you function out of a sense of wholeness and happiness, there is practically nothing on earth which can stop you from achieving the great sense of inner rejoicing and victory which is yours to enjoy as a citizen of this magnificent cosmos.

The divine aspect of existence resides within us, but it is only when we are grateful towards it that we can bring ourselves to the tremendous experience of clarity and sanity. Arjun's mind is veering towards an insane state: he has become so confused and his thoughts have become so clouded, that he is tottering as if he is a drunk person. He's not able to experience the heartbeat of his own being in a manner which brings delight; in a manner which brings clarity and lucid understanding of the situation. And Krishna is simply bringing the lucidity of understanding to Arjun. He's making Arjun hear that which he needs to hear, and so doing brings him very swiftly to a state where Arjun is able to really imbibe the message of the Master.

There transpires in the Gita a deep energy between the Master and the disciple, which breaks down Arjun's ego but also fills him with a courage which is beyond the ordinary. And when you are filled with a courage beyond the ordinary, then only can you gather up enough sanity within yourself to be able to utilize your life energy to the fullest. Otherwise most of us are utilizing our life energy in a very partial way, simply because our thoughts are clouding us with all sorts of fears and doubts—much as Arjun's own mind was clouded with thoughts and doubts. So really the thing is to slip out of this cycle of vicious thought, and to understand yourself as a presence which is comprised of clear consciousness. Then do you attain the universal message which Krishna is talking about. This universal message is about feeling a divine contentment in life. And divine contentment in life is not about contentment with 'things', but rather with a state of being. And the only way you can attain a state of being which is truly contented is to discover that sheer joy which comes out of psychological clarity. When the psychology is clear, then actions too become clear. Emotions become clear, feelings become clear. And all that was disturbing you at the subtle or gross levels stop having impact on you. You become free of bondages and become your most dynamic self!

CHAPTER-24

You Are No One, Yet Are Universal in Spirit: Lesson for Spiritually Inspired Leadership

LESSON: Hidden within you is universal energy and power. Never underestimate that: it is always with you. You are a reflection of the highest divine principle that Krishna represents. This is His teaching to Arjun: that on the one hand every mortal being is insignificant, yet is cosmic also, due to the hidden dimension of the divine within! Understanding this is the inner key to inspired living and leadership.

There is a very mystic aspect of the Gita which illustrates how none of us is really important in the cosmic scheme of things, but how at the same time we have an innate value *(mulya)*. A timeless and eternal significance in the vastness of existence, though in a small way.

What Krishna does is bring Arjun to his knees by showing him the glory and splendour of His universal form. By explaining the vastness of existence, Krishna makes Arjun extremely humble. Suddenly, this mighty warrior and mighty leader of men—this iconic person for mankind, Arjun—is reduced to having to surrender to the cosmic principle. But at the same time, Krishna also shows Arjun that He dwells within him as the indwelling spirit; that the essence of the Lord is available to Arjun. In other words, Krishna demonstrates that while on the one hand Arjun (and indeed none of us) is nothing at all in the cosmic scheme of things (we are just a small speck of dust on a planet which is also just a speck of dust in the vastness of existence), at the same time the glory of the Infinite is always with us! This glory is always accessible to us. Through this understanding, Arjun is completely transformed! It instils humility, but with a deep confidence that even as a very humble part of existence we have infinite riches. We have infinite power. We have infinite capacity as human beings, as doers of action or as leaders in whatever field we are involved in.

The whole journey of the Bhagavad Gita and the whole effort of Krishna is to make us understand that while at the circumference of one's being we can be doing any action, but that action itself is meaningless unless we know the centre of our beings. The centre within which dwells the truly significant power of the cosmic—that is what would give us a deep sense of comprehending the vastness of ourselves. While at the same time understanding that no matter how much respect we have from others and no matter how much people defer to our position of power, wealth, or outward riches, it is always the inner riches which matter. A person who undergoes this understanding comes to realize that he is not superior or inferior to anybody, but that what makes him unique is his own individual realization of the inner treasure of spirit. And so doing, dynamism comes into the human mind and soul.

Understand that light of the Infinite is like a fire within your souls. When you understand the light of the greater, the force of the Infinite within yourself, then comes great dynamism into whatever you do. You become a guiding light, a pathfinder, who can take not only yourself but others too out of darkness. And essentially that is what a leader is meant to do: take people out of the darkness of crisis and problems. Good leadership implies the ability to take people out of tense situations and circumstances, out of the darkness of worry and anxiety. And to make them rejoice in mind, dance at heart, with hope and positivity. Where there is hope and positivity, there comes the abundance of life.

So a good leader prepares the ground for such positivity and optimism. He tills the soil of human aspiration, so to speak, and on that soil all that you plant can flourish. But the very basis of the soil lies within an objective realization of the greatness of innate spirit. Without that objective realization of the greatness of spirit, true confidence does not arise in a person.

Often, the confidence of leaders is fake, not from their inner being. It could be projected or borrowed from their position, from their followers, from their wealth, and so on. But real confidence is that of a person who might be without anything, but still has the light and radiance of spirit shining through in whatever he or she does. A good example in the modern era would be Swami Vivekananda. There is a very poignant first-hand description by HJ Van Haagen who describes Vivekananda as being someone 'whose walk expressed dignity and whole general bearing showed majesty, like one who owns everything and desires nothing.' This is the description of a spiritually realized true leader of mankind. What it means is that a real pathfinder is not necessarily possessive or ambitious to get a material reward—who is rather simple—but who's very demeanour talks of an inner confidence! And this inner confidence shines through in all she or he does. So such a person becomes a natural leader of men. And this is the universal rule: that if we realize the spirit, there comes about a radiance of our outer being. Which is why all sorts of mystics throughout history have been shown with a 'halo' around themselves. They were very radiant in their manner and demeanour. It seems like they're emitting a light of inner, deep hope and confidence. And that shows up as an illumination of their being! Wherever they go, people feel lit up with their presence. That is real charisma. The Rishis have been portrayed with this halo, the avatars in Hinduism have been portrayed with this halo. Gautam Buddha has been portrayed with this halo, so too Jesus Christ, Zarathustra, Guru Nanak, Mahavir, the Sufis, and so on.

If you can feel great integration and unity within your inner being, there comes about an organic growth and manifestation of your personality into whatever you do as a leader. You become prepared to lead people unto new and greater shores. Yet without this feeling of deep unity with spirit or the Supreme within you, you can never develop true and abiding confidence.

We are all bound to be dust eventually. The only thing which abides is that mind-stream, that consciousness, which we have come with and which endures in the mystic dimension. The subtle part of us exists timelessly, the material part is bound to get destroyed. And this is what Krishna constantly reminds Arjun.

In a strange way, a person like Steve Jobs shows us some glimpses of what this understanding means for a leader who has an interest in the mystical and spiritual. Jobs' own personal needs were very simple: his home was sparsely decorated, he hardly owned any possessions, he was not a person who liked to accumulate symbols of wealth. He was rather simple in his demeanour. His way of dressing was very simple: a black turtleneck T-shirt and jeans. He used to drive a simple car; he just had a music system at home and very few possessions. Yet there was an inner passion when it came to his work! There was a deep inner passion when it came to his sense of aesthetics! His mission was to do something which would abide for humanity; to use technology for a purpose which was creative, and which could help people become more creative. So he reflects *spiritually inspired leadership*. It's not being possessive about material things at the individual level, yet about realizing the spirit of things, and having passion for this sense of spirit. It manifests as creativity. It could manifest as a service or a product for society. But the essential basis of it is not a pursuit of personal possessions, yet always a pursuit of something higher than that! And this is what makes truly great leaders.

CHAPTER - 25

Live Joyfully!

LESSON: Don't let your inner peace and joy be shaken even when it looks like events outside have shaken the world! This becomes key in the scenario of catastrophes such as war, calamities, and mass-scale epidemics! Maintain equilibrium within, and out of that arises a naturally joyful energy. Nourish that energy and create a synthesis of mind-body-soul power within yourself. Arjun suffers due to the disturbance of his inner joyful synthesis; once he regains that, he becomes capable of meeting all challenges, and becomes once again the great warrior-leader that he is!

One of the most important lessons from the Gita is that life is to be lived with great joy, with great cheer in one's heart. And not to be lived in the darkness of anxiety. As an internal quality within leaders, it is a crucial lesson: only those who can experience deep states of joy can truly work towards creating joy for others! The ultimate function of a good leader is to lead people and society to joyful fulfilment and success. That can only happen when they are themselves inwardly luminous with a vibe of joyful vigour/energy. Cheerfulness is key for leaders and not only keeps them creatively inspired, but influences levels of passion throughout the organization they lead.

The greater truth that Krishna is conveying to Arjun is that all is comprised ultimately of great bliss and great joy. And that no matter what our circumstances in life are, it is our bounden spiritual duty to enlighten our consciousness with this feeling of joy. Then everything in our life becomes joyful.

Arjun's problem is that he's in a deep inner agony; he's in a struggle and conflict within himself. His mind is very far away from the joyous state. His mind is very far away from the state of contentment. Krishna makes him realize that, ultimately, all that Arjun can do is to bring himself to a great state of mental equilibrium and mental joy. When that happens, whatever he does—whether he wins the battle or loses it, whether he kills his enemies or is killed by them—he can accept joyously, gracefully. And this transforms Arjun's consciousness entirely. Where he was anxious, he starts becoming joyful.

So the whole secret is becoming joyful: this creates a great awareness within the consciousness. It creates a great alertness of being. It creates a state where you are alive to the whisper of the Lord's message to you within the deepest part of your mind.

All of us are living in a great cosmic miracle, a great universal splendour. But very few of us experience the bliss to be enjoyed within it! We don't wonder about it. We are so perturbed by our own problems that the greater joy of life is missed altogether. And that is the greatest waste of human energy and of human life.

We become mentally impotent in a state of anxiety: Arjun acts like an absolutely powerless person in the beginning of the Gita. But as Krishna gives him the lesson of joyful living, Arjun finds that he can accept everything with a great deal of intelligence, with a great deal of awareness. And, most importantly, with a great deal of bliss within his heart. And when this bliss within his heart suffuses his being, he arises and fights as he should: as a true mystic warrior. His fight is for justice, and there is nothing to be so sorrowful about it!

The whole of the Gita is a gospel for joyful living. If you can understand this, then you'd really know the essence of the Gita itself. This whole universe is itself in a great state of rejoicing to the command of the procreating divine energy! This creative Power brings all things into existence, and suffuses them with bliss.

We simply have to stop identifying with our anxieties. We have to stop identifying with our circumstances and our sufferings. We have to be a little detached. When you become a little detached is when you can become joyful. You don't even need to move towards 'enlightenment'; joy and bliss themselves catalyse the movement toward human enlightenment. Then inner purity comes about spontaneously, our inner quality of consciousness shines brighter as a by-product of the state of joy. Then you'd never feel alone in the world. Arjun is feeling a great sense of aloneness. He is feeling a great sense of moving towards death in this forlorn aloneness. But Krishna explains to him that what we perceive life to be is really part of a great cosmic cycle. It is moving at a very high speed, a very high velocity, and is dictated not by our whims and fancies but by the far greater infinite universal power. Hence our attitude in life should simply be joyful. Our attitude towards life and death both should be joyful. There is nothing to grieve for; there is nothing to be sorrowful for: it is all part of our greater reality. And that greater reality puts us at ease, if only we accept its functioning, if only we accept that we are to flow with the natural cosmic order of things. Then our consciousness starts becoming a reflection of universal bliss itself. Our ego dies in this attitude. And when the ego dies, then we become absolutely full of a divine consciousness. A great fragrance engulfs us, and we are able to make life into a great dance of our soul.

What is the essence of religion? The 'religion' of the Gita is the religion of joy. It is not a question of ritual at all. Rather, it is to awaken one's consciousness to this inner state of joy. Then all things become possible. Because if the consciousness is touched by this joyfulness, then you really know the invisible part of life. The problem is, we get so bogged down by the visible part and the material part, that we forget there is a spiritual bliss always available to us. The door of eternity is always available to us. And we can enter it if we have joy and bliss within us. It is timeless. It is a dimension which has no attributes. It is transcendent to all material situations. That is what the essence of religion is according to the Gita. And if we go deeply into it, we will find that this creates a sense of infiniteness in our lives. Else, we are living very limited lives. We are emotionally so caught up in our problems that we identify with them. And being identified, we get caught up in their complexities. Be detached! Be a little profound in your outlook, be a little calm in your outlook. And then you'll find the art of turning the negative also into something tremendously useful. You will find that you have within you the ability to ring the bells of the heart as you wish. The only quality required is the light of joy: it takes you towards a higher truth, a higher liberation, a higher freedom of being and a higher intelligence.

You become joined with the ecstasy of the absolute when you feel ecstasy within yourself. The microcosm is a reflection of the macrocosm, especially when it comes to this ability to feel joy—because that is the universal substance. That is the *Ananda*, that is the Bliss which pervades all things! Krishna's Gita is extremely transformative of Arjun's consciousness. It takes him from a psychological situation of great depression, to a psychological situation of great joyful dynamism. In that state of being Arjun can act as he's meant to act: as the true warrior. He becomes an instrument, as it were, of the Lord's work within the world. And we are all just instruments that Nature has created for a certain purpose. We must allow its greater functioning to work through us. And the best way to channel its greater functioning is by simply identifying not with anxieties and problems as much as we do with the joyful and blissful state—because that is our ultimate reality. That is what takes us beyond the limitations of our present circumstances and to a state of tremendous fearlessness, tremendous calmness, tremendous love within ourselves. It creates a state of passion in being, and where there is passion in being all aspects of our life become transformed: our work, our relationships, our ability to succeed in the world.

So the real secret is this, and only this: that life is to be lived joyfully. If we know this, we would grasp the essence of the religious path which the Gita is professing.

The whole objective of the Gita is to make Arjun realize the inner treasure within himself. And that inner treasure is the divine element which is playing out throughout the cosmos. Ordinarily, we are unconscious of it, but the state of joy makes us realize it and become one with it. Hence, it is the religious state. Hence, the ecstatic state is really the closest state to God-realization and self-realization, because it takes us towards unknown shores of the infinite. It gives us a fragrance of peace which we do not ordinarily feel by any material accomplishments. It is by itself totally apart from accumulating power, money, and so on. It is an accumulation of true riches. It takes us from feeling that we are nothing to feeling that we are everything . . . and that is what happens to Arjun.

In the beginning of the Gita, we can see that Arjun feels like a nobody. He feels that he's absolutely insignificant. He feels like he is in fact an instrument of destruction. However, as the Gita progresses, Krishna conveys powerfully to him that there is tremendous value within each individual, but that value only comes about when we allow the Greater to function through us. And the Greater likes nothing better than that we realize—with great ananda or bliss—our inherent divine consciousness. Identify with the ecstasy that is divine consciousness. That is the way to revolutionize your life. That is the perfection of being. That is what encircles the heart and mind with a great energy! It dynamizes our soul. At the level of body, mind, and spirit, it creates a situation where all sadness evaporates. And all our problems seem solvable. You see, man ordinarily perceived life as a series of problems to be solved. Each day can seem like a burden: there's so much to do, so many 'problems' to solve. There's so much to accomplish. Remember that it is always the state of cheerfulness which brings us back to realizing the divine element within life. And when that happens, you are able to transform your whole being from one of darkness to one of inner light!

Arjun has gone into a very darkened, depressive state. He feels like his freedom to act or his dynamism to act has been snatched away by the troubles of his mind. The anxieties and doubts that his mind have, make him feel burdened. But it is actually good that he has doubts and anxieties: else, the gospel of bliss, the gospel of joy called the Gita would not have been taught to him by the Lord! So, yes, it is very important for us to reflect upon our anxieties or sadness, but never to wallow in them. Realize that the gospel is available to us. Also realize that the message of the Lord can ring true within our own heart.

The essence of the Gita is always available to us through our inner state of joy. It gives us a power ad infinitum, which allows us great spiritual growth. It gives us the eyes to see that everything is in great ecstasy: the way the planets and galaxies are revolving, the simple beauty of flowers and birds, the magical change of seasons, the dew drop on the leaf during dawn . . . All things are in a deep ecstasy, joined to the Lord. Only man has become detached from this cosmic and universal joy. Joy is the sweetest thing; it is the most fragrant thing. Hence, remember that it is very important to non-identify with our anxious moments; through non-identification with anxiety comes the recognition of that flame of ecstasy which is ever alive within the deepest recesses of our mind. Knowing it, you can never be anxious, you can never feel alone. Knowing it, you feel centred, integrated, and strong. And that makes you move forward with a great deal of confidence and inner power. Then, whatever task you touch in the outer world also becomes transformed as a result of it.

The greatest way of dynamic living is that of blissful living. There is no substitute for it. The very experience of joy creates a great crystallization of inner power and strength within you. It takes you from the ordinary to the extraordinary, from the conscious to the super-conscious, from the mundane to the sacred, from the human to the divine. It is the very essence of the Gita. In a way, it is opposite to the law of gravitation. The law of gravitation pulls us towards earth; it keeps us grounded. The law of joy gives us spiritual wings to fly to the greater truth, to the ecstasy of our highest selves. It is a platform, a foundation, a stepping-stone to the greatest realization of our own potential.

It enables the fruition of the highest leadership values: integrity, bold decision-making, charismatic confidence-creation, trustworthiness, crisis aversion via being more aware and alert of the broader dimensions of all things.

CHAPTER - 26

Resurrection of Consciousness

LESSON: The secret of the Gita lies in its power to renew us with inner power, hope, optimism, and strength. It helps us give birth to these qualities and re-awaken them every time we are feeling low, just as Arjun was. The Gita is the ultimate leadership manual in this sense, because the most crucial leadership attributes are indeed inner power, hope, optimism, and strength of consciousness.

In the eastern spiritual concepts, true spirituality means the ability to completely leave behind our old patterns of consciousness. Implying being reborn in consciousness. Implying a resurrection. The whole Gita is a process of rebirth for Arjun. It is the death of his old concepts. The death of his old mind. The Gita is Arjun's resurrection. It enables him to come out of his internal personal crisis—as every leader should—and deal with the external material crisis in the best manner possible.

Regarding this point, a fundamental difference in the understanding of Eastern and Western religions is very important: when Christianity travelled to the West from the Middle East, the concept of Christ's 'resurrection' was mistaken to be that on the physical plane—the literal resurrection of Jesus. But really what it implies is the resurrection of consciousness. And in the Gita, this is very clearly seen. It is a great lesson, a great secret which needs to be emphasized more and more as far as the Gita goes. In fact, as far as all of religion goes!

Arjun's mind is being absolutely freshly created through the teachings of the Gita. The old mind of his is shattered by the dynamic teachings of Krishna. The principle of resurrection, the principle of harmonizing and crystallizing a new consciousness within Arjun, is the whole vibe of the Gita. That is its ultimate grace. That is its ultimate sensibility. It is a movement from the old way of thinking—that we are bounded, limited, finite—and unto the new understanding that we are part of the infinite. That we are part of something far greater than we ever thought.

Arjun is told by Krishna very clearly to leave behind all

that he previously held to be true, and to surrender to the higher principle. This is also very important and practical for our day-to-day lives. Most of us are conditioned due to our old thought patterns and our old way of looking at things. And this also implies that our same old anxieties, doubts, and so on, keep plaguing us. What is the way out? The way out is, as Krishna tells Arjun, to completely move out of the fear that he is feeling! To move out of the anxiety that he's feeling. To move out of the disturbed state of consciousness that he has been feeling so far in his life. And when the mind becomes new, fresh, when the consciousness is able to look at things in a fresh light, then it catalyses the presence of the divine within us! It provokes the presence of our highest potentiality.

Then our lives become full of a great, loving energy, full of a great courageous energy. And through the action of this energy, our entire life becomes transformed—not just at the intellectual or logical level, but from the very roots of our psycho-spiritual being.

Hence, this concept of spiritual resurrection is really important for us to understand. Krishna-consciousness or Christ-consciousness are really the ability to move out of the old consciousness. Then only is the consciousness of the higher available to us. Then only can we move into bliss. Then only can we move to our greatest heights.

Yes, Krishna is telling Arjun to perform his duty:

the same duty as a warrior that he always performed, but now he will do it with a mind that has been reborn! Shedding the old just like a snake sheds its old skin and emerges afresh. So too is the human being to throw away the deeply rooted concepts within the mind; to come out of that skin of all thoughts and emerge with a real root-energy of newness and freshness in perception. This is the ultimate learning, for it takes us to the deepest depths of our inner being. It allows us to see the beauty of life, the majesty of our own existence . . . and brings all our powers and energies to the greatest flowering. For it allows us to come into the state where we open our eyes and remove all limitations, all barriers, all boundaries around ourselves. And free our minds.

Arjun is freeing his mind. This is just another way of saying that he is rebirthing his mind, he is being reborn in mind. Arjun had kept on clinging to the thoughts that were plaguing him, but by clinging to thoughts we are never able to move on. In that state, we are never able to move on to our self-realization of potential. Neither are we able to move on beyond sorrow, beyond anxiety, and so on. And moving on is really the key!

Move forward! That is the very essence of mysticism. That is the very essence of spirituality. That is the quality of dynamism. Arjun has come into a state where he feels that he is in mental darkness, there is lethargy in will. It is a state of *tamasic* energy. And then the wisdom of the Gita is lighted within him! The *rajasic* energy of action and the *sattvic* energy of spiritual knowledge is ignited within him. The dynamism, the balance is found.

You cannot aspire to balance without leaving behind old fears. Only when you do that, can you face up to the new with a newness of courage. So it is exceedingly important not just for our own well-being and peace of mind, but also in order to cultivate the most luminous part of ourselves—at the level of mind, body, and soul. It is then that we attain a new vision of life.

Attaining a new vision of life is real resurrection. Attaining a new vision of life is the rebirth! And that is what the whole Bhagavad Gita is about. Krishna is making Arjun move on to a whole new vision of life. And through this newness of vision comes about purity, as a by-product and as a spontaneous happening. Arjun becomes free; Arjun becomes able to glimpse into the higher truth of reality. He is able to vibrate with the immense energy of the warrior that he is, once again!

So, it is all about quality of energy. If you keep harkening back to old thoughts and old things, your quality of energy will never emerge fresh. You will always be in a state of split mind: the state of schizophrenia. Half your mind will be caught up in the old and half of it will be trying to deal with new circumstances. Hence, being obsessed with the past is really what creates mental agony. To move towards a coolness of mind, to move towards a divine light, it is very important that we cleanse ourselves. Take a mental shower, as it were! Stand under the waterfall and let the waters cleanse you . . . and that is what the Gita is. It is this cleansing Ganges of the mind. It is this cleansing waterfall of the consciousness. It is this fresh flow of the river. If you put your foot into a river, you can never touch the same water twice: it keeps flowing, and fresh water keeps coming. And that creates its own delight! It has its own dynamism, its own movement, its own energy. So too the mind should be in a state of flow. The mind should be able to move into a situation where it can get past its embedded and conditioned anxieties. That is what psychologists also say. That is what the whole basis of psychoanalysis is, in fact.

So the Gita is very dynamic in this way. It is not at all in conflict with modern psychoanalysis; in fact, it is a much, much more advanced form of it! Because it deals with all the hidden factors of life as well. It deals with that 'x-factor' which we may call the universal force, the cosmic force, and so on, of which we are but a part. It does not look at the human being only as comprised of a body and mind, but also looks at him as a universal citizen. As a being located within the wonder of the vast universe and hence an intrinsic spiritual part of it too.

The Gita looks at the human being as an unlimited being, a cosmic citizen, and hence includes the deep mystical angle of being human. And that is the way the Gita tells us to look at life: with the mystic eye. If we understand this, we are able to move on from the old! We become really rich in our consciousness. Else, we remain rather poor in our way of looking at life.

Mental opulence is the ability to go past the old. Mental poverty means to get frozen in old concepts; to get frozen in conditioned thoughts and anxieties, and so on. The whole idea is to flow more freely. The whole idea is to use the creative power of flowing energy within you! And that creative energy is constantly taking you towards the divine. It is constantly taking you towards fulfilment and contentment. Keep flowing, keep moving on . . . Do not become stagnant. Arjun has become stagnant on the battlefield. And stagnation is basically so pernicious that it has made Arjun absolutely helpless. The great warrior has been reduced to a weakling! And, in fact, what really creates a weakling out of us is this tendency to keep clinging to the old. Wisdom implies that you absolutely drop and let go of all that has been hindering you.

The soul needs to be stirred in an unending flow: that is the whole science of human dynamism. And there's nothing more eloquent than the Gita to express this. It suffuses us with bliss, because it takes us to an absolute emptying of all our old concepts. An emptying of our old thoughts. And fills in place of that a spontaneity of flowing energy. That is what happens to Arjun: he becomes spontaneously joyful, content, full of wonder through the course of the Gita. He finds his answers. And that is the root of self-confidence.

Arjun had become totally under-confident of himself. In fact, his confidence had been shattered. But by the end of Krishna's discourse, his self-confidence grows to such an extent that it is no longer about ego, but is about surrendering to the larger power that runs the universe. Through the process, Arjun finds creativity, energy, courage infinite. And the greatest bliss enters his mind: that is the Bliss of the infinite. The absolute. There is no bliss comparable to it. Arjun drops the old ideas of the mind and moves to a situation where he is absolutely reborn and resurrected into a timeless space.

Time is only a concept: it is possible for the human mind to transcend the concept of time, if only we identify ourselves with the larger infinite power that runs things! Of which all things are part of as a flow. If we keep identifying with our anxious minds, we never come into that situation. The whole idea is to dissolve into the vaster reality. And that is what Arjun's mind does eventually: it dissolves into the vaster reality that Krishna has shown it.

And through that, it comes to a situation where it finds its own dance, its own eternal happiness.

The happiness of the mind can never be achieved by repetitive thought. The happiness of the mind lies in freshness; it lies in feeling new. It lies in feeling wonder. It lies in perceiving things with new eyes of vision. Only in that do you move towards the state of enlightenment. Else, you continue to wallow in darkness through the thoughts that the anxious mind keeps suggesting.

Do not weaken yourself by identifying with shallow anxious thoughts: go beyond them. Then the transformation happens! That is the path of the creative person, the courageous person. It is the path of Arjun. And he is lucky to have the Lord Himself direct him on this path.

The whole idea is an acceptance of whatever has happened, and to move on with that acceptance. To become happy; not through identifying with thought, but through freeing oneself from all prisons of thought! By freeing oneself from one's own self-imposed limitations of mind! By freeing oneself in the mystical dimensions of being. And through that, encountering a greater awareness, a greater bliss, a greater opportunity to feel like you can move to the next level of living. And that level of living is that of super-consciousness. You are to attain a higher consciousness, just as Arjun does through the Gita. The inner eye of his is activated. He matures; he is able to go past the content of the old mind, and thereby revolutionize himself in a way that the cosmic energy begins dancing within him once again. And he is able to fulfil his Dharma, his duty as a warrior, to the best extent possible.

By doing this, Arjun ensures that as a key leadership icon/luminary and warrior-prince, he sets the right example. And being a great leadership example is key. As Krishna tells Arjun: 'Whatever a great person does, others follow.'

Acknowledgements

I wish to express my humble gratitude to the people who have made this series possible:

Anuj Bahri, my super literary agent at Red Ink.

Shikha Sabharwal and Gaurav Sabharwal, my wonderful publishers at Fingerprint! Publishing and their team.

Garima Shukla, my amazing and brilliant editor.

Family—my parents, partner Sohini, sister Priti, nieces, nephews, et al: you are my rock.

Gratitude also to my support team, friends, mentors, and well-wishers over the years.

Pranay is a mystic philosopher. He is an expert on Indian and world spirituality.

Pranay's modules on 'Advanced Spirituality for Leadership and Success' (PowerTalks/MysticTalks for public and corporate audiences) have won global acclaim.

Pranay is also a theatre personality and playwright. His original productions such as *From Kabir to Kavi* and *Soul Stir* have been acclaimed by world luminaries for their path-breaking spiritual content.

Pranay and his partner Sohini run the socio-cultural philanthropic commune TAS, whose initiatives such as 'Theatre Against Drugs' (for addicts), 'Geetimalya' (for underprivileged children) and 'Shohaag' (for women empowerment) are well-known and have become movements.

Presently, Pranay is collating his discourses on mind-body-spirit themes for various book series.

Connect with him on his website: pranay.org